Paul Auster was born in New Jersey in 1947. After attending Columbia University he lived in France for four years. Since 1974 he has published poems, essays, novels and translations. He lives in Brooklyn, New York.

The Red Notebook

and other writings

━━

PAUL AUSTER

faber and faber

LONDON · BOSTON

This edition first published in 1995
by Faber and Faber Limited
3 Queen Square London WC1N 3AU
Open market paperback edition first published in 1995
This UK paperback edition first published in 1996

The pieces in this collection (except for 'A Prayer for Salman Rushdie')
appeared in *The Art of Hunger*, first published in the USA in 1992 by Sun
and Moon Press, and in 1993 by Penguin Books. A shorter edition of *The
Art of Hunger* was published by Menard Press (London) in 1982.
'Twentieth-Century French Poetry' was first printed in *The Random House
Book of Twentieth-Century French Poetry* (New York: Random House, 1982);
'Mallarmé's Son' was first printed in *A Tomb for Anatole* by Stephane
'Mallarmé (San Francisco: North Point Press, 1983). 'A Prayer for Salman
Rushdie' was first printed in *The New York Times*. 'Why Write' first
appeared in *The New Yorker*.

Phototypeset by Intype, London
Printed in England by Clays Ltd, St Ives plc

A CIP record for this book is available from the British Library

ISBN 0-571-17433-7

2 4 6 8 10 9 7 5 3 1

CONTENTS

I

The Red Notebook

1

In 1972 a close friend of mine ran into trouble with the law. She was in Ireland that year, living in a small village not far from the town of Sligo. As it happened, I was visiting on the day a plainclothes detective drove up to her cottage and presented her with a summons to appear in court. The charges were serious enough to require a lawyer. My friend asked around and was given a name, and the next morning we bicycled into town to meet with this person and discuss the case. To my astonishment, he worked for a firm called Argue and Phibbs.

This is a true story. If there are those who doubt me, I challenge them to visit Sligo and see for themselves if I have made it up or not. I have reveled in these names for the past twenty years, but even though I can prove that Argue and Phibbs were real men, the fact that the one name should have been coupled with the other (to form an even more delicious joke, an out-and-out sendup of the legal profession) is something I still find hard to believe.

According to my latest information (three or four years ago), the firm continues to do a thriving business.

The following year (1973), I was offered a job as caretaker of a farmhouse in the south of France. My friend's legal troubles were well behind her, and since our on-again off-again romance seemed to be on again, we decided to join forces and take the job together. We had both run out of money by then, and without this offer we would have been compelled to return to America – which neither one of us was prepared to do just yet.

It turned out to be a curious year. On the one hand, the place was beautiful: a large, eighteenth-century stone house bordered by vineyards on one side and a national forest on the other. The nearest village was two kilometers away, but it was inhabited by no more than forty people, none of whom was under sixty or seventy years old. It was an ideal spot for two young writers to spend a year, and L. and I both worked hard there, accomplishing more in that house than either one of us would have thought possible.

On the other hand, we lived on the brink of permanent catastrophe. Our employers, an American couple who lived in Paris, sent us a small monthly salary (fifty dollars), a gas allowance for the car, and money to feed the two Labrador retrievers who were part of the household. All in all, it was a generous arrangement. There was no rent to pay, and even if our salary fell short of what we needed to live on, it gave us a head start on each month's expenses. Our plan was to earn the rest by doing translations. Before leaving Paris and settling in the country, we had set up a number of jobs to see us through the year. What we had neglected to take into account was that publishers are often slow to pay their bills. We had also forgotten to consider that checks sent from one country to another can take weeks to clear, and that once they do, bank charges and exchange fees cut into the amounts of those checks. Since L. and I had left no margin for error or miscalculation, we often found ourselves in quite desperate straits.

I remember savage nicotine fits, my body numb with need as I scrounged among sofa cushions and crawled behind cupboards in search of loose coins. For eighteen centimes (about three and a half cents), you could buy a brand of cigarettes called Parisiennes, which were sold in packs of four. I remember feeding the dogs and thinking that they ate better than I did. I remember conversations with L. when we seriously considered opening a can of dog food and eating it for dinner.

Our only other source of income that year came from a man named James Sugar. (I don't mean to insist on metaphorical names, but facts are facts, and there's nothing I can do about it.) Sugar worked as a staff photographer for *National Geographic*, and he entered our lives because he was collaborating with one of our employers on an article about the region. He took pictures for several months, crisscrossing Provence in a rented car provided by his magazine, and whenever he was in our neck of the woods he would spend the night with us. Since the magazine also provided him with an expense account, he would very graciously slip us the money that had been allotted for his hotel costs. If I remember correctly, the sum came to fifty francs a night. In effect, L. and I became his private innkeepers, and since Sugar was an amiable man into the bargain, we were always glad to see him. The only problem was that we never knew when he was going to turn up. He never called in advance, and more often than not weeks would go by between his visits. We therefore learned not to count on Mr. Sugar. He would arrive out of nowhere, pulling up in front of the house in his shiny blue car, stay for a night or two, and then disappear again. Each time he left, we assumed that was the last time we would ever see him.

The worst moments came for us in the late winter and early spring. Checks failed to arrive, one of the dogs was stolen, and little by little we ate our way through the stockpile of food in the kitchen. In the end, we had nothing left but a bag of onions, a bottle of cooking oil, and a packaged pie crust that someone had bought before we ever moved into the house – a stale remnant from the previous summer. L. and I held out all morning and into the afternoon, but by two-thirty hunger had gotten the better of us, and so we went into the kitchen to prepare our last meal. Given the paucity of elements we had to work with, an onion pie was the only dish that made sense.

After our concoction had been in the oven for what seemed a sufficient length of time, we took it out, set it on the table, and dug in. Against all our expectations, we both found it delicious. I think we even went so far as to say that it was the best food we had ever tasted, but no doubt that was a ruse, a feeble attempt to keep our spirits up. Once we had chewed a little more, however, disappointment set in. Reluctantly – ever so reluctantly – we were forced to admit that the pie had not yet cooked through, that the center was still too cold to eat. There was nothing to be done but put it back in the oven for another ten or fifteen minutes. Considering how hungry we were, and considering that our salivary glands had just been activated, relinquishing the pie was not easy.

To stifle our impatience, we went outside for a brief stroll, thinking the time would pass more quickly if we removed ourselves from the good smells in the kitchen. As I remember it, we circled the house once, perhaps twice. Perhaps we drifted into a deep conversation about something (I can't remember), but however it happened, and however long we were gone, by the time we entered the house again the kitchen was filled with smoke. We rushed to the oven and pulled out the pie, but it was too late. Our meal was dead. It had been incinerated, burned to a charred and blackened mass, and not one morsel could be salvaged.

It sounds like a funny story now, but at the time it was anything but funny. We had fallen into a dark hole, and neither one of us could think of a way to get out. In all my years of struggling to be a man, I doubt there has ever been a moment when I felt less inclined to laugh or crack jokes. This was really the end, and it was a terrible and frightening place to be.

That was at four o'clock in the afternoon. Less than an hour later, the errant Mr. Sugar suddenly appeared, driving up to the house in a cloud of dust, gravel and dirt crunching all around him. If I think about it hard enough, I can still see the naive and goofy smile on his face as he bounced out of the car and said hello. It was a miracle. It was a genuine miracle, and I was there to witness it with my own eyes, to live it in my own flesh. Until that moment, I had thought those things happened only in books.

Sugar treated us to dinner that night in a two-star restaurant. We ate copiously and well, we emptied several bottles of wine, we laughed our heads off. And yet, delicious as that food must have been, I can't remember a thing about it. But I have never forgotten the taste of the onion pie.

3

Not long after I returned to New York (July 1974), a friend told me the following story. It is set in Yugoslavia, during what must have been the last months of the Second World War.

S.'s uncle was a member of a Serbian partisan group that fought against the Nazi occupation. One morning, he and his comrades woke up to find themselves surrounded by German troops. They were holed up in a farmhouse somewhere in the country, a foot of snow lay on the ground, and there was no escape. Not knowing what else to do, the men decided to draw lots. Their plan was to burst out of the farmhouse one by one, dash through the snow, and see if they couldn't make it to safety. According to the results of the draw, S.'s uncle was supposed to go third.

He watched through the window as the first man ran out into the snow-covered field. There was a barrage of machine-gun fire from across the woods, and the man was cut down. A moment later, the second man ran out, and the same thing happened. The machine guns blasted, and he fell down dead in the snow.

Then it was my friend's uncle's turn. I don't know if he hesitated at the doorway, I don't know what thoughts were pounding through his head at that moment. The only thing I was told was that he started to run, charging through the

9

snow for all he was worth. It seemed as if he ran forever. Then, suddenly, he felt pain in his leg. A second after that, an overpowering warmth spread through his body, and a second after that he lost consciousness.

When he woke up, he found himself lying on his back in a peasant's cart. He had no idea how much time had elapsed, no idea of how he had been rescued. He had simply opened his eyes – and there he was, lying in a cart that some horse or mule was pulling down a country road, staring up at the back of a peasant's head. He studied the back of that head for several seconds, and then loud explosions began to erupt from the woods. Too weak to move, he kept looking at the back of the head, and suddenly it was gone. It just flew off the peasant's body, and where a moment before there had been a whole man, there was now a man without a head.

More noise, more confusion. Whether the horse went on pulling the cart or not I can't say, but within minutes, perhaps even seconds, a large contingent of Russian troops came rolling down the road. Jeeps, tanks, scores of soldiers. When the commanding officer took a look at S.'s uncle's leg, he quickly dispatched him to an infirmary that had been set up in the neighbourhood. It was no more than a rickety wooden shack – a henhouse, maybe, or an outbuilding on some farm. There the Russian army doctor pronounced the leg past saving. It was too severely damaged, he said, and he was going to have to cut it off.

My friend's uncle began to scream. 'Don't cut off my leg,' he cried. 'Please, I beg of you, don't cut off my leg!' But no one listened to him. The medics strapped him to the operating table, and the doctor picked up the saw. Just as he was about to pierce the skin of the leg, there was another explosion. The roof of the infirmary collapsed, the walls fell down, the entire place was obliterated. And once again, S.'s uncle lost consciousness.

When he woke up this time, he found himself lying in a bed. The sheets were clean and soft, there were pleasant smells in the room, and his leg was still attached to his body. A moment later, he was looking into the face of a beautiful young woman. She was smiling at him and feeding him broth with a spoon. With no knowledge of how it had happened, he had been rescued again and carried to another farmhouse. For several minutes after coming to, S.'s uncle wasn't sure if he was alive or dead. It seemed possible to him that he had woken up in heaven.

He stayed on in the house during his recovery and fell in love with the beautiful young woman, but nothing ever came of that romance. I wish I could say why, but S. never filled me in on the details. What I do know is that his uncle kept his leg – and that once the war was over, he moved to America to begin a new life. Somehow or other (the circumstances are obscure to me), he wound up as an insurance salesman in Chicago.

4

L. and I were married in 1974. Our son was born in 1977, but by the following year our marriage had ended. None of that is relevant now – except to set the scene for an incident that took place in the spring of 1980.

We were both living in Brooklyn then, about three or four blocks from each other, and our son divided his time between the two apartments. One morning, I had to stop by L.'s house to pick up Daniel and walk him to nursery school. I can't remember if I went inside the building or if Daniel came down the stairs himself, but I vividly recall that just as we were about to walk off together, L. opened the window of her third-floor apartment to throw me some money. Why she did that is also forgotten. Perhaps she wanted me to replenish a parking meter for her, perhaps I was supposed to do an errand, I don't know. All that remains is the open window and the image of a dime flying through the air. I see it with such clarity, it's almost as if I have studied photographs of that instant, as if it's part of a recurring dream I've had ever since.

But the dime hit the branch of a tree, and its downward arc into my hand was disrupted. It bounced off the tree, landed soundlessly somewhere nearby, and then it was gone. I remember bending down and searching the pavement, digging among the leaves and twigs at the base of the tree, but the dime was nowhere to be found.

I can place that event in early spring because I know that later the same day I attended a baseball game at Shea Stadium – the opening game of the season. A friend of mine had been offered tickets, and he had generously invited me to go along with him. I had never been to an opening game before, and I remember the occasion well.

We arrived early (something about collecting the tickets at a certain window), and as my friend went off to complete the transaction, I waited for him outside one of the entrances to the stadium. Not a single soul was around. I ducked into a little alcove to light a cigarette (a strong wind was blowing that day), and there, sitting on the ground not two inches from my feet, was a dime. I bent down, picked it up, and put it in my pocket. Ridiculous as it might sound, I felt certain that it was the same dime I had lost in Brooklyn that morning.

5

In my son's nursery school, there was a little girl whose parents were going through a divorce. I particularly liked her father, a struggling painter who earned his living by doing architectural renderings. His paintings were quite beautiful, I thought, but he never had much luck in convincing dealers to support his work. The one time he did have a show, the gallery promptly went out of business.

B. was not an intimate friend, but we enjoyed each other's company, and whenever I saw him I would return home with renewed admiration for his steadfastness and inner calm. He was not a man who grumbled or felt sorry for himself. However gloomy things had become for him in recent years (endless money problems, lack of artistic success, threats of eviction from his landlord, difficulties with his ex-wife), none of it seemed to throw him off course. He continued to paint with the same passion as ever, and unlike so many others, he never expressed any bitterness or envy towards less talented artists who were doing better than he was.

When he wasn't working on his own canvasses, he would sometimes go to the Metropolitan Museum and make copies of the old masters. I remember a Caravaggio he once did that struck me as utterly remarkable. It wasn't a copy so much as a replica, an exact duplication of the original. On one of those visits to the museum, a Texas millionaire spotted B. at work and was so impressed that he commissioned him to do a copy of a Renoir painting – which he then presented to his fiancée as a gift.

B. was exceedingly tall (six-five or six-six), good-looking, and gentle in his manner – qualities that made him especially attractive to women. Once his divorce was behind him and he began to circulate again, he had no trouble finding female companions. I only saw him about two or three times a year, but each time I did, there was another woman in his life. All of them were obviously mad for him. You had only to watch them looking at B. to know how they felt, but for one reason or another, none of these affairs lasted very long.

After two or three years, B.'s landlord finally made good on his threats and evicted him from his loft. B. moved out of the city, and I lost touch with him.

Several more years went by, and then one night B. came back to town to attend a dinner party. My wife and I were also there, and since we knew that B. was about to get married, we asked him to tell us the story of how he had met his future wife.

About six months earlier, he said, he had been talking to a friend on the phone. This friend was worried about him, and after a while he began to scold B. for not having married again. You've been divorced for seven years now, he said, and in that time you could have settled down with any one of a dozen attractive and remarkable women. But no one is ever good enough for you, and you've turned them all away. What's wrong with you, B.? What in the world do you want?

There's nothing wrong with me, B. said. I just haven't found the right person, that's all.

At the rate you're going, you never will, the friend

answered. I mean, have you ever met one woman who comes close to what you're looking for? Name one. I dare you to name just one.

Startled by his friend's vehemence, B. paused to consider the question carefully. Yes, he finally said, there was one. A woman by the name of E., whom he had known as a student at Harvard more than twenty years ago. But she had been involved with another man at the time, and he had been involved with another woman (his future ex-wife), and nothing had developed between them. He had no idea where E. was now, he said, but if he could meet someone like her, he knew he wouldn't hesitate to get married again.

That was the end of the conversation. Until mentioning her to his friend, B. hadn't thought about this woman in over ten years, but now that she had resurfaced in his mind, he had trouble thinking about anything else. For the next three or four days, he thought about her constantly, unable to shake the feeling that his one chance for happiness had been lost many years ago. Then, almost as if the intensity of these thoughts had sent a signal out into the world, the phone rang one night, and there was E. on the other end of the line.

B. kept her on the phone for more than three hours. He scarcely knew what he said to her, but he went on talking until past midnight, understanding that something momentous had happened and that he mustn't let her escape again.

After graduating from college, E. had joined a dance company, and for the past twenty years she had devoted herself exclusively to her career. She had never married, and now that she was about to retire as a performer, she was calling old friends from her past, trying to make contact with the world again. She had no family (her parents had been killed in a car crash when she was a small girl) and had been raised by two aunts, both of whom were now dead.

B. arranged to see her the next night. Once they were together, it didn't take long for him to discover that his feelings for her were just as strong as he had imagined. He fell in love with her all over again, and several weeks later they were engaged to be married.

To make the story even more perfect, it turned out that E. was independently wealthy. Her aunts had been rich, and after they died she had inherited all their money – which meant that not only had B. found true love, but the crushing money problems that had plagued him for so many years had suddenly vanished. All in one fell swoop.

A year or two after the wedding, they had a child. At last report, mother, father, and baby were doing just fine.

6

In much the same spirit, although spanning a shorter period of time (several months as opposed to twenty years), another friend, R., told me of a certain out-of-the-way book that he had been trying to locate without success, scouring bookstores and catalogues for what was supposed to be a remarkable work that he very much wanted to read, and how, one afternoon as he made his way through the city, he took a shortcut through Grand Central Station, walked up the staircase that leads to Vanderbilt Avenue, and caught sight of a young woman standing by the marble railing with a book in front of her: the same book he had been trying so desperately to track down.

Although he is not someone who normally speaks to strangers, R. was too stunned by the coincidence to remain silent. 'Believe it or not,' he said to the young woman, 'I've been looking everywhere for that book.'

'It's wonderful', the young woman answered. 'I just finished reading it.'

'Do you know where I could find another copy?' R. asked. 'I can't tell you how much it would mean to me.'

'This one is for you,' the woman answered.

'But it's yours,' R. said.

'It *was* mine,' the woman said, 'but now I'm finished with it. I came here today to give it to you.'

7

Twelve years ago, my wife's sister went off to live in Taiwan. Her intention was to study Chinese (which she now speaks with breathtaking fluency) and to support herself by giving English lessons to native Chinese speakers in Taipei. That was approximately one year before I met my wife, who was then a graduate student at Columbia University.

One day, my future sister-in-law was talking to an American friend, a young woman who had also gone to Taipei to study Chinese. The conversation came around to the subject of their families back home, which in turn led to the following exchange:

'I have a sister who lives in New York,' my future sister-in-law said.

'So do I,' her friend answered.

'My sister lives on the Upper West Side.'

'So does mine.'

'My sister lives on West 109th Street.'

'Believe it or not, so does mine.'

'My sister lives at 309 West 109th Street.'

'So does mine!'

'My sister lives on the second floor of 309 West 109th Street.'

The friend took a deep breath and said, 'I know this sounds crazy, but so does mine.'

It is scarcely possible for two cities to be farther apart than Taipei and New York. They are at opposite ends of the earth, separated by a distance of more than ten thousand miles, and when it is day in one it is night in the other. As the two young women in Taipei marveled over the astounding connection they had just uncovered, they realized that their two sisters were probably asleep at that moment. On the same floor of the same building in northern Manhattan, each one was sleeping in her own apartment, unaware of the conversation that was taking place about them on the other side of the world.

Although they were neighbors, it turned out that the two sisters in New York did not know each other. When they finally met (two years later), neither one of them was living in that building anymore.

Siri and I were married then. One evening, on our way to an appointment somewhere, we happened to stop in at a bookstore on Broadway to browse for a few minutes. We must have wandered into different aisles, and because Siri wanted to show me something, or because I wanted to show her something (I can't remember), one of us spoke the other's name out loud. A second later, a woman came rushing up to us. 'You're Paul Auster and Siri Hustvedt, aren't you?' she said. 'Yes,' we said, 'that's exactly who we are. How did you know that?' The woman then explained that her sister and Siri's sister had been students together in Taiwan.

The circle had been closed at last. Since that evening in the bookstore ten years ago, this woman has been one of our best and most loyal friends.

8

Three summers ago, a letter turned up in my mailbox. It came in a white oblong envelope and was addressed to someone whose name was unfamiliar to me: Robert M. Morgan of Seattle, Washington. Various post office markings were stamped across the front: *Not Deliverable, Unable to Forward, Return to Writer*. Mr. Morgan's name had been crossed out with a pen, and beside it someone had written *Not at this address*. Drawn in the same blue ink, an arrow pointed to the upper left-hand corner of the envelope, accompanied by the words *Return to sender*. Assuming that the post office had made a mistake, I checked the upper left-hand corner to see who the sender was. There, to my absolute bewilderment, I discovered my own name and my own address. Not only that, but this information was printed on a custom-made address label (one of those labels you can order in packs of two hundred from advertisements on matchbook covers). The spelling of my name was correct, the address was my address – and yet the fact was (and still is) that I have never owned or ordered a set of printed address labels in my life.

Inside, there was a single-spaced typewritten letter that began: 'Dear Robert, In response to your letter dated July 15, 1989, I can only say that, like other authors, I often receive letters concerning my work.' Then, in a bombastic, pretentious style, riddled with quotations from French philosophers and oozing with a tone of conceit and self-satisfaction, the letter-writer went on to praise 'Robert' for the ideas he had developed about one of my books in a college course on the contemporary novel. It was a contemptible letter, the kind of letter I would never dream of writing to anyone, and yet it was signed with my name. The handwriting did not resemble mine, but that was small comfort. Someone was out there trying to impersonate me, and as far as I know he still is.

One friend suggested that this was an example of 'mail art.' Knowing that the letter could not be delivered to Robert Morgan (since there was no such person), the author of the letter was actually addressing his remarks to me. But that would imply an unwarranted faith in the U.S. Postal Service, and I doubt that someone who would go to the trouble of ordering address labels in my name and then sitting down to write such an arrogant, high-flown letter would leave anything to chance. Or would he? Perhaps the smart alecks of this world believe that everything will always go their way.

I have scant hope of ever getting to the bottom of this little mystery. The prankster did a good job of covering his tracks, and he has not been heard from since. What puzzles me about my own behavior is that I have not thrown away the letter, even though it continues to give me chills every time I look at it. A sensible man would have tossed the thing in the garbage. Instead, for reasons I do not understand, I have kept it on my work table for the past three years, allowing it to become a permanent fixture among my pens and notebooks and erasers. Perhaps I keep it there as a monument to my own folly. Perhaps it is a way to remind myself that I know nothing, that the world I live in will go on escaping me forever.

9

One of my closest friends is a French poet by the name of C. We have known each other for more than twenty years now, and while we don't see each other often (he lives in Paris and I live in New York), the bond between us remains strong. It is a fraternal bond, somehow, as if in some former life we had actually been brothers.

C. is a man of manifold contradictions. He is both open to the world and shut off from it, a charismatic figure with scores of friends everywhere (legendary for his kindness, his humor, his sparkling conversation) and yet someone who has been wounded by life, who struggles to perform the simple tasks that most other people take for granted. An exceptionally gifted poet and thinker about poetry, C. is nevertheless hampered by frequent writing blocks, streaks of morbid self-doubt, and surprisingly (for someone who is so generous, so profoundly lacking in mean-spiritedness), a capacity for long-standing grudges and quarrels, usually over some trifle or abstract principle. No one is more universally admired than C., no one has more talent, no one so readily commands the center of attention, and yet he has always done everything in his power to marginalize himself. Since his separation from his wife many years ago, he has lived alone in a number of small, one-room apartments, subsisting on almost no money and only fitful bouts of employment, publishing little, and refusing to write a single word of criticism, even though he reads everything and knows more about contemporary poetry than anyone in France. To those of us who love him (and we are many), C. is often a cause of concern. To the degree that we respect him and care about his well-being, we also worry about him.

He had a rough childhood. I can't say to what extent that explains anything, but the facts should not be overlooked. His father apparently ran off with another woman when C. was a little boy, and after that my friend grew up with his mother, an only child with no family life to speak of. I have never met C.'s mother, but by all accounts she is a bizarre character. She went through a series of love affairs during C.'s childhood and adolescence, each with a man younger than the man before him. By the time C. left home to enter the army at the age of twenty-one, his mother's boyfriend was scarcely older than he was. In more recent years, the central purpose of her life has been a campaign to promote the canonization of a certain Italian priest (whose name eludes me now). She has besieged the Catholic authorities with countless letters defending the holiness of this man, and at one point she even commissioned an artist to create a life-size statue of the priest – which now stands in her front yard as an enduring testament to her cause.

Although not a father himself, C. became a kind of pseudo-father seven or eight years ago. After a falling out with his girlfriend (during which they temporarily broke up), his girlfriend had a brief affair with another man and became pregnant. The affair ended almost at once, but she decided to have the baby on her own. A little girl was born, and even though C. is not her real father, he has devoted himself to her since the day of her birth and adores her as if she were his own flesh and blood.

One day about four years ago, C. happened to be visiting a friend. In the apartment there was a *Minitel*, a small computer given out free by the French telephone company. Among other things, the *Minitel* contains the address and phone number of every person in France. As C. sat there playing with his friend's new machine, it suddenly occurred to him to look up his father's address. He found it in Lyon. When he returned home later that day, he stuffed one of his books into an envelope and sent it off to the address in Lyon – initiating the first contact with his father in over forty years. None of it made any sense to him. Until he found himself doing these things, it had never even crossed his mind that he wanted to do them.

That same night, he ran into another friend in a café – a woman psychoanalyst – and told her about these strange, unpremeditated acts. It was as if he had felt his father calling out to him, he said, as if some uncanny force had unleashed itself inside him. Considering that he had absolutely no memories of the man, he couldn't even begin to guess when they had last seen each other.

The woman thought for a moment and said, 'How old is L.?' referring to C.'s girlfriend's daughter.

'Three and a half,' C. answered.

'I can't be sure,' the woman said, 'but I'd be willing to bet that you were three and a half the last time you saw your father. I say that because you love L. so much. Your identification with her is very strong, and you're reliving your life through her.'

Several days after that, there was a reply from Lyon – a warm and perfectly gracious letter from C.'s father. After thanking C. for the book, he went on to tell him how proud he was to learn that his son had grown up to become a writer. By pure coincidence, he added, the package had been mailed on his birthday, and he was very moved by the symbolism of the gesture.

None of this tallied with the stories C. had heard throughout his childhood. According to his mother, his father was a monster of selfishness who had walked out on her for a 'slut' and had never wanted anything to do with his son. C. had believed these stories, and therefore he had shied away from any contact with his father. Now, on the strength of this letter, he no longer knew what to believe.

He decided to write back. The tone of his response was guarded, but nevertheless it was a response. Within days he received another reply, and this second letter was just as warm and gracious as the first had been. C. and his father began a correspondence. It went on for a month or two, and eventually C. began to consider traveling down to Lyon to meet his father face to face.

Before he could make any definite plans, he received a letter from his father's wife informing him that his father was dead. He had been in ill health for the past several years, she wrote, but the recent exchange of letters with C. had given him great happiness, and his last days had been filled with optimism and joy.

It was at this moment that I first heard about the incredible reversals that had taken place in C.'s life. Sitting on the train from Paris to Lyon (on his way to visit his 'stepmother' for the first time), he wrote me a letter that sketched out the story of the past month. His handwriting reflected each jolt of the tracks, as if the speed of the train were an exact image of the thoughts racing through his head. As he put it somewhere in that letter: 'I feel as if I've become a character in one of your novels.'

His father's wife could not have been friendlier to him

during that visit. Among other things, C. learned that his father had suffered a heart attack on the morning of his last birthday (the same day that C. had looked up his address on the *Minitel*) and that, yes, C. had been precisely three and a half years old at the time of his parents' divorce. His stepmother then went on to tell him the story of his life from his father's point of view – which contradicted everything his mother had ever told him. In this version, it was his mother who had walked out on his father; it was his mother who had forbidden his father from seeing him; it was his mother who had broken his father's heart. She told C. how his father would come around to the schoolyard when he was a little boy to look at him through the fence. C. remembered that man, but not knowing who he was, he had been afraid.

C.'s life had now become two lives. There was Version A and Version B, and both of them were his story. He had lived them both in equal measure, two truths that cancelled each other out, and all along, without even knowing it, he had been stranded in the middle.

His father had owned a small stationery store (the usual stock of paper and writing materials, along with a rental library of popular books). The business had earned him a living, but not much more than that, and the estate he left behind was quite modest. The numbers are unimportant, however. What counts is that C.'s stepmother (by then an old woman) insisted on splitting the money with him half and half. There was nothing in the will that required her to do that, and morally speaking she needn't have parted with a single penny of her husband's savings. She did it because she wanted to, because it made her happier to share the money than to keep it for herself.

In thinking about friendship, particularly about how some friendships endure and others don't, I am reminded of the fact that in all my years of driving I have had just four flat tires, and that on each of these occasions the same person was in the car with me (in three different countries, spread out over a period of eight or nine years). J. was a college friend, and though there was always an edge of unease and conflict in our relations, for a time we were close. One spring while we were still undergraduates, we borrowed my father's ancient station wagon and drove up into the wilderness of Quebec. The seasons change more slowly in that part of the world, and winter was not yet over. The first flat tire did not present a problem (we were equipped with a spare), but when a second tire blew out less than an hour later, we were stranded in the bleak and frigid countryside for most of the day. At the time, I shrugged off the incident as a piece of bad luck, but four or five years later, when J. came to France to visit the house where L. and I were working as caretakers (in miserable condition, inert with depression and self-pity, unaware that he was overstaying his welcome with us), the same thing happened. We went to Aix-en-Provence for the day (a drive of about two hours), and coming back later that night on a dark, back-country road, we had another flat. Just a coincidence, I thought, and then pushed the event out of my mind. But then, four years after that, in the waning months of my marriage to L., J. came to visit us again – this time in New York State, where L. and I were living with the infant Daniel. At one point, J. and I climbed into the car to go to the store and shop for dinner. I pulled the car out of the garage, turned it around in the rutted dirt driveway, and advanced to the edge of the road to look left, right, and left before going on. Just then, as I waited for a car to pass by, I heard the unmistakable hiss of escaping air. Another tire had gone flat, and this time we hadn't even left the house. J. and I both laughed, of course, but the truth is that our friendship never really recovered from that fourth flat tire. I'm not saying that the flat tires were responsible for our drifting apart, but in some perverse way they were an emblem of how things had always stood between us, the sign of some impalpable curse. I don't want to exaggerate, but even now I can't quite bring myself to reject those flat tires as meaningless. For the fact is that J. and I have lost contact, and we have not spoken to each other in more than ten years.

In 1990, I found myself in Paris again for a few days. One afternoon, I stopped by the office of a friend to say hello and was introduced to a Czech woman in her late forties or early fifties – an art historian who happened to be a friend of my friend. She was an attractive and vivacious person, I remember, but since she was on the point of leaving when I walked in, I spent no more than five or ten minutes in her company. As usually happens in such situations, we talked about nothing of any importance: a town we both knew in America, the subject of a book she was reading, the weather. Then we shook hands, she walked out the door, and I have never seen her again.

After she was gone, the friend I had come to visit leaned back in her chair and said, 'Do you want to hear a good story?'

'Of course,' I said. 'I'm always interested in good stories.'

'I like my friend very much,' she continued, 'so don't get the wrong idea. I'm not trying to spread gossip about her. It's just that I feel you have a right to know this.'

'Are you sure?'

'Yes, I'm sure. But you have to promise me one thing. If you ever write the story, you mustn't use anyone's name.'

'I promise,' I said.

And so my friend let me in on the secret. From start to

finish, it couldn't have taken her more than three minutes to tell the story I am about to tell now.

The woman I had just met was born in Prague during the war. When she was still a baby, her father was captured, impressed into the German army, and shipped off to the Russian front. She and her mother never heard from him again. They received no letters, no news to tell them if he was alive or dead, nothing. The war just swallowed him up, and he vanished without a trace.

Years passed. The girl grew up. She completed her studies at the university and became a professor of art history. According to my friend, she ran into trouble with the government during the Soviet crackdown in the late sixties, but exactly what kind of trouble was never made clear to me. Given the stories I know about what happened to other people during that time, it is not very difficult to guess.

At some point, she was allowed to begin teaching again. In one of her classes, there was an exchange student from East Germany. She and this young man fell in love, and eventually they were married.

Not long after the wedding, a telegram arrived announcing the death of her husband's father. The next day, she and her husband traveled to East Germany to attend the funeral. Once there, in whatever town or city it was, she learned that her now dead father-in-law had been born in Czechoslovakia. During the war he had been captured by the Nazis, impressed into the German army, and shipped off to the Russian front. By some miracle, he had managed to survive. Instead of returning to Czechoslovakia after the war, however, he had settled in Germany under a new name, had married a German woman, and had lived there with his new family until the day of his death. The war had given him a chance to start all over again, and it seems that he had never looked back.

When my friend's friend asked what this man's name had been in Czechoslovakia, she understood that he was her father.

Which meant, of course, that insofar as her husband's father was the same man, the man she had married was also her brother.

One afternoon many years ago, my father's car stalled at a red light. A terrible storm was raging, and at the exact moment his engine went dead, lightning struck a large tree by the side of the road. The trunk of the tree split in two, and as my father struggled to get the car started again (unaware that the upper half of the tree was about to fall), the driver of the car behind him, seeing what was about to happen, put his foot on the accelerator and pushed my father's car through the intersection. An instant later, the tree came crashing to the ground, landing in the very spot where my father's car had just been. What was very nearly the end of him proved to be no more than a close call, a brief episode in the ongoing story of his life.

A year or two after that, my father was working on the roof of a building in Jersey City. Somehow or other (I wasn't there to witness it), he slipped off the edge and started falling to the ground. Once again, he was headed for certain disaster, and once again he was saved. A clothesline broke his fall, and he walked away from the accident with only a few bumps and bruises. Not even a concussion. Not a single broken bone.

That same year, our neighbors across the street hired two men to paint their house. One of the workers fell off the roof and was killed.

The little girl who lived in that house happened to be my sister's best friend. One winter night, the two of them went to a costume party (they were six or seven years old, and I was nine or ten). It had been arranged that my father would pick them up after the party, and when the time came I went along to keep him company in the car. It was bitter cold that night, and the roads were covered with treacherous sheets of ice. My father drove carefully, and we made the journey back and forth without incident. As we pulled up in front of the little girl's house, however, a number of unlikely events occurred all at once.

My sister's friend was dressed as a fairy princess. To complete the outfit, she had borrowed a pair of her mother's high heels, and because her feet swam in those shoes, every step she took was turned into an adventure. My father stopped the car and climbed out to accompany her to the front door. I was in the back with the girls, and in order to let my sister's friend out, I had to get out first. I remember standing on the curb as she disentangled herself from the seat, and just as she stepped into the open air, I noticed that the car was rolling slowly in reverse – either because of the ice or because my father had forgotten to engage the emergency brake (I don't know) – but before I could tell my father what was happening, my sister's friend touched the curb with her mother's high heels and slipped. She went skidding under the car – which was still moving – and there she was, about to be crushed to death by the wheels of my father's Chevy. As I remember it, she didn't make a sound. Without pausing to think, I bent down from the curb, grabbed hold of her right hand, and in one quick gesture yanked her to the sidewalk. An instant later, my father finally noticed that the car was moving. He jumped back into the driver's seat, stepped on the brake, and brought the machine to a halt. From start to finish, the whole chain of misadventures couldn't have taken more than eight or ten seconds.

For years afterward, I walked around feeling that this had been my finest moment. I had actually saved someone's life, and in retrospect I was always astonished by how quickly I had acted, by how sure my movements had been at the critical juncture. I saw the rescue in my mind again and again; again and again I relived the sensation of pulling that little girl out from under the car.

About two years after that night, our family moved to another house. My sister fell out of touch with her friend, and I myself did not see her for another fifteen years.

It was June, and my sister and I had both come back to town for a short visit. Just by chance, her old friend dropped by to say hello. She was all grown up now, a young woman of twenty-two who had graduated from college earlier that month, and I must say that I felt some pride in seeing that she had made it to adulthood in one piece. In a casual sort of way, I mentioned the night I had pulled her out from under the car. I was curious to know how well she remembered her brush with death, but from the look on her face when I asked the question, it was clear that she remembered nothing. A blank stare. A slight frown. A shrug. She remembered nothing!

I realized then that she hadn't known the car was moving. She hadn't even known that she was in danger. The whole incident had taken place in a flash: ten seconds of her life, an interval of no account, and none of it had left the slightest mark on her. For me, on the other hand, those seconds had been a defining experience, a singular event in my internal history.

Most of all, it stuns me to acknowledge that I am talking about something that happened in 1956 or 1957 – and that the little girl of that night is now over forty years old.

13

My first novel was inspired by a wrong number. I was
alone in my apartment in Brooklyn one afternoon, sitting
at my desk and trying to work when the telephone rang.
If I am not mistaken, it was the spring of 1980, not many
days after I found the dime outside Shea Stadium.

I picked up the receiver, and the man on the other end
asked if he was talking to the Pinkerton Agency. I told him
no, he had dialed the wrong number, and hung up. Then
I went back to work and promptly forgot about the call.

The next afternoon, the telephone rang again. It turned
out to be the same person asking the same question I had
been asked the day before: 'Is this the Pinkerton Agency?'
Again I said no, and again hung up. This time, however, I
started thinking about what would have happened if I had
said yes. What if I had pretended to be a detective from
the Pinkerton Agency? I wondered. What if I had actually
taken on the case?

To tell the truth, I felt that I had squandered a rare
opportunity. If the man ever called again, I told myself, I
would at least talk to him a little bit and try to find out
what was going on. I waited for the telephone to ring
again, but the third call never came.

After that, wheels started turning in my head, and little
by little an entire world of possibilities opened up to me.

When I sat down to write *City of Glass* a year later, the wrong number had been transformed into the crucial event of the book, the mistake that sets the whole story in motion. A man named Quinn receives a phone call from someone who wants to talk to Paul Auster, the private detective. Just as I did, Quinn tells the caller he has dialed the wrong number. It happens again the next night, and again Quinn hangs up. Unlike me, however, Quinn is given another chance. When the phone rings again on the third night, he plays along with the caller and takes on the case. Yes, he says, I'm Paul Auster – and at that moment the madness begins.

Most of all, I wanted to remain faithful to my original impulse. Unless I stuck to the spirit of what had really happened, I felt there wouldn't have been any purpose to writing the book. That meant implicating myself in the action of the story (or at least someone who resembled me, who bore my name), and it also meant writing about detectives who were not detectives, about impersonation, about mysteries that cannot be solved. For better or worse, I felt I had no choice.

All well and good. I finished the book ten years ago, and since then I have gone on to occupy myself with other projects, other ideas, other books. Less than two months ago, however, I learned that books are never finished, that it is possible for stories to go on writing themselves without an author.

I was alone in my apartment in Brooklyn that afternoon, sitting at my desk and trying to work when the telephone rang. This was a different apartment from the one I had in 1980 – a different apartment with a different telephone number. I picked up the receiver, and the man on the other end asked if he could speak to Mr. Quinn. He had a Spanish accent and I did not recognize the voice. For a moment I thought it might be one of my friends trying to pull my leg. 'Mr. Quinn?' I said. 'Is this some kind of joke or what?'

No, it wasn't a joke. The man was in dead earnest. He had to talk to Mr. Quinn, and would I please put him on the line. Just to make sure, I asked him to spell out the name. The caller's accent was quite thick, and I was hoping that he wanted to talk to Mr. Queen. But no such luck. 'Q-U-I-N-N,' the man answered. I suddenly grew scared, and for a moment or two I couldn't get any words out of my mouth. 'I'm sorry,' I said at last, 'there's no Mr. Quinn here. You've dialed the wrong number.' The man apologized for disturbing me, and then we both hung up.

This really happened. Like everything else I have set down in this red notebook, it is a true story.

1992

II

Prefaces

1

French and English constitute a single language.
Wallace Stevens

This much is certain: if not for the arrival of William and his armies on English soil in 1066, the English language as we know it would never have come into being. For the next three hundred years French was the language spoken at the English court, and it was not until the end of the Hundred Years' War that it became clear, once and for all, that France and England were not to become a single country. Even John Gower, one of the first to write in the English vernacular, composed a large portion of his work in French, and Chaucer, the greatest of the early English poets, devoted much of his creative energy to a translation of *Le Roman de la rose* and found his first models in the work of the Frenchman Guillaume de Machaut. It is not simply that French must be considered an 'influence' on the development of English language and literature; French is a part of English, an irreducible element of its genetic make-up.

Early English literature is replete with evidence of this symbiosis, and it would not be difficult to compile a lengthy catalogue of borrowings, homages and thefts. William Caxton, for instance, who introduced the printing press in

England in 1477, was an amateur translator of medieval French works, and many of the first books printed in Britain were English versions of French romances and tales of chivalry. For the printers who worked under Caxton, translation was a normal and accepted part of their duties, and even the most popular English work to be published by Caxton, Thomas Malory's *Morte d'Arthur*, was itself a ransacking of Arthurian legends from French sources: Malory warns the reader no less than fifty-six times during the course of his narrative that the 'French book' is his guide.

In the next century, when English came fully into its own as a language and a literature, both Wyatt and Surrey – two of the most brilliant pioneers of English verse – found inspiration in the work of Clément Marot, and Spenser, the major poet of the next generation, not only took the title of his *Shepheardes Calender* from Marot, but two sections of the work are direct imitations of that same poet. More importantly, Spenser's attempt at the age of seventeen to translate Joachim du Bellay (*The Visions of Bellay*) is the first sonnet sequence to be produced in English. His later revision of that work and translation of another du Bellay sequence, *Ruines of Rome*, were published in 1591 and stand among the great works of the period. Spenser, however, is not alone in showing the mark of the French. Nearly all the Elizabethan sonnet writers took sustenance from the Pléiade poets, and some of them – Daniel, Lodge, Chapman – went so far as to pass off translations of French poets as their own work. Outside the realm of poetry, the impact of Florio's translation of Montaigne's essays on Shakespeare has been well documented, and a good case could be made for establishing the link between Rabelais and Thomas Nashe, whose 1594 prose narrative, *The Unfortunate Traveler*, is generally considered to be the first novel written in the English language.

On the more familiar terrain of modern literature, French has continued to exert a powerful influence on English. In spite of the wonderfully ludicrous remark by Southey that poetry is as impossible in French as it is in Chinese, English and American poetry of the past hundred years would be inconceivable without the French. Beginning with Swinburne's 1862 article in *The Spectator* on Baudelaire's *Les Fleurs du Mal* and the first translations of Baudelaire's poetry into English in 1869 and 1870, modern British and American poets have continued to look to France for new ideas. Saintsbury's article in an 1875 issue of *The Fortnightly Review* is exemplary. 'It was not merely admiration of Baudelaire which was to be persuaded to English readers,' he wrote, 'but also imitation of him which, at least with equal earnestness, was to be urged on English writers.'

Throughout the 1870s and 1880s, largely inspired by Théodore de Banville, many English poets began experimenting with French verse forms (ballades, lays, virelays and rondeaux), and the 'art for art's sake' ideas propounded by Gautier were an important source for the Pre-Raphaelite movement in England. By the 1890s, with the advent of *The Yellow Book* and the Decadents, the influence of the French Symbolists became widespread. In 1893, for example, Mallarmé was invited to lecture at Oxford, a sign of the esteem he commanded in English eyes.

It is also true that little of substance was produced in English as a result of French influences during this period, but the way was prepared for the discoveries of two young American poets, Pound and Eliot, in the first decade of the new century. Each came upon the French independently, and each was inspired to write a kind of poetry that had not been seen before in English. Eliot would later write that ' . . . the kind of poetry I needed, to teach me the use of my own voice, did not exist in England at all, and was only to be found in France.' As for Pound, he stated flatly that 'practically the whole development of the English verse-art has been achieved by steals from the French.'

The English and American poets who formed the Imagist group in the years just prior to World War I were the first to engage in a *critical* reading of French poetry, with the aim not so much of imitating the French as of rejuvenating poetry in English. More or less neglected poets in France, such as Corbière and Laforgue, were accorded major status. F. S. Flint's 1912 article in *The Poetry Review* (London) and Ezra Pound's 1913 article in *Poetry* (Chicago) did much to promote this new reading of the French. Independent of the Imagists, Wilfred Owen spent several years in France before the war and was in close contact with Laurent Tailhade, a poet admired by Pound and his circle. Eliot's reading of the French poets began as early as 1908, while he was still a student at Harvard. Just two years later he was in Paris, reading Claudel and Gide and attending Bergson's lectures at the Collège de France.

By the time of the Armory show in 1913, the most radical tendencies in French art and writing had made their way to New York, finding a home with Alfred Stieglitz and his gallery at 291 Fifth Avenue. Many of the names associated with American and European modernism became part of this Paris-New York connection: Joseph Stella, Marsden Hartley, Arthur Dove, Charles Demuth, William Carlos Williams, Man Ray, Alfred Kreymborg, Marius de Zayas, Walter C. Arensberg, Mina Loy, Francis Picabia and Marcel Duchamp. Under the influence of Cubism and Dada, of Apollinaire and the Futurism of Marinetti, numerous magazines carried the message of modernism to American readers: *291*, *The Blind Man*, *Rongwrong*, *Broom*, *New York Dada*, and *The Little Review*, which was born in Chicago in 1914, lived in New York from 1917 to 1927, and died in Paris in

1929. To read the list of *The Little Review*'s contributors is to understand the degree to which French poetry had permeated the American scene. In addition to work by Pound, Eliot, Yeats and Ford Madox Ford, as well as its most celebrated contribution, James Joyce's *Ulysses*, the magazine published Breton, Eluard, Tzara, Péret, Reverdy, Crevel, Aragon and Soupault.

Beginning with Gertrude Stein, who arrived in Paris well before World War I, the story of American writers in Paris during the twenties and thirties is almost identical to the story of American writing itself. Hemingway, Fitzgerald, Faulkner, Sherwood Anderson, Djuna Barnes, Kay Boyle, e e cummings, Hart Crane, Archibald MacLeish, Malcolm Cowley, John Dos Passos, Katherine Anne Porter, Laura Riding, Thornton Wilder, Williams, Pound, Eliot, Glenway Wescott, Henry Miller, Harry Crosby, Langston Hughes, James T. Farrell, Anaïs Nin, Nathanael West, George Oppen – all of these and others either visited or lived in Paris. The experience of those years has so thoroughly saturated American consciousness that the image of the starving young writer serving his apprenticeship in Paris has become one of our enduring literary myths.

It would be absurd to assume that each of these writers was directly influenced by the French. But it would be just as absurd to assume that they went to Paris only because it was a cheap place to live. In the most serious and energetic magazine of the period, *transition*, American and French writers were published side by side, and the dynamics of this exchange led to what has probably been the most fruitful period in our literature. Nor does absence from Paris necessarily preclude an interest in things French. The most Francophilic of all our poets, Wallace Stevens, never set foot in France.

Since the twenties, American and British poets have been

steadily translating their French counterparts – not simply as a literary exercise, but as an act of discovery and passion. Consider, for example, these words from John Dos Passos's preface to his translations of Cendrars in 1930: ' ... A young man just starting to read verse in the year 1930 would have a hard time finding out that this method of putting words together has only recently passed through a period of virility, intense experimentation and meaning in everyday life ... For the sake of this hypothetical young man and for the confusion of Humanists, stuffed shirts in editorial chairs, anthology compilers and prize poets, sonnet writers and readers of bookchats, I think it has been worth while to attempt to turn these alive informal personal everyday poems of Cendrars' into English ... ' Or T. S. Eliot, introducing his translation of *Anabasis* by Saint-John Perse that same year: 'I believe that this is a piece of writing of the same importance as the later work of James Joyce, as valuable as *Anna Livia Plurabelle*. And this is a high estimate indeed.' Or Kenneth Rexroth, in the preface to his translations of Reverdy in 1969: 'Of all the modern poets in Western European languages Reverdy has certainly been the leading influence in my own work – incomparably more than anyone in English or American – and I have known and loved his work since I first read *Les Épaves du ciel* as a young boy.'

As the list of translators included in this book shows, many of the most important contemporary American and British poets have tried their hand at translating the French, among them Pound, Williams, Eliot, Stevens, Beckett, Mac-Neice, Spender, Ashbery, Blackburn, Bly, Kinnell, Levertov, Merwin, Wright, Tomlinson, Wilbur – to mention just some of the most familiar names. It would be difficult to imagine their work had they not been touched in some way by the French. And it would be even more difficult to imagine the poetry of our own language if these poets had not been a part of it. In a sense, then, this anthology is as much about American and British poetry as it is about French poetry. Its purpose is not only to present the work of French poets in French, but to offer translations of that work as our own poets have re-imagined and re-presented it. As such, it can be read as a chapter in our own poetic history.

2

The French tradition and the English tradition in this epoch are at opposite poles to each other. French poetry is more radical, more total. In an absolute and exemplary way it has assumed the heritage of European Romanticism, a romanticism which begins with William Blake and the German romantics like Novalis, and via Baudelaire and the Symbolists culminates in twentieth-century French poetry, notably Surrealism. It is a poetry where the world becomes writing and language becomes the double of the world.

Octavio Paz

On the other hand, this much is also certain: if there has been a steady interest in French poetry for the past hundred years on the part of British and American poets, enthusiasm for the French has often been tempered by a certain wariness, even hostility, to literary and intellectual practices in France. This has been more true of the British than the Americans, but, nevertheless, the American literary establishment remains strongly Anglophilic in orientation. One has only to compare the dominant trends in philosophy, literary criticism, or novel-writing to realize the enormous gulf between the two cultures.

Many of these differences reside in the disparities between the two languages. Although English is in large part derived from French, it still holds fast to its Anglo-Saxon origins. Against the gravity and substantiality to be found in the work of our greatest poets (Milton, say, or Emily Dickinson), which embodies an awareness of the contrast between the thick emphasis of Anglo-Saxon and the nimble conceptuality of French/Latin – and to play one repeatedly against the other – French poetry often seems almost weightless to us, to be composed of ethereal puffs of lyricism and little else. French is necessarily a thinner medium than English. But that does not mean it is weaker. If English writing has staked out as its territory the world of tangibility, of concrete presence, of surface accident, French literary language has largely been a language of essences. Whereas Shakespeare, for example, names more than five hundred flowers in his plays, Racine adheres to the single word 'flower'. In all, the French dramatist's vocabulary consists of roughly fifteen hundred words, while the word count in Shakespeare's plays runs upward of twenty-five thousand. The contrast, as Lytton Strachey noted, is between 'comprehension' and 'concentration'. 'Racine's great aim,' Strachey wrote, 'was to produce, not an extraordinary nor a complex work of art, but a flawless one; he wished to be all matter and no impertinence. His conception of a drama was of something swift, inevitable; an action taken at the crisis, with no redundancies however interesting, no complications however suggestive, no irrelevances however beautiful – but plain, intense, vigorous, and splendid with nothing but its own essential force.' More recently, the poet Yves Bonnefoy has described English as a 'mirror' and French as a 'sphere', the one Aristotelian in its acceptance of the given, the other Platonic in its readiness to hypothesize 'a different reality, a different realm'.

Samuel Beckett, who has spent the greater part of his life writing in both languages, translating his own work from French into English and from English into French, is no doubt our most reliable witness to the capacities and limitations of the two languages. In one of his letters from the mid-fifties, he complained about the difficulty he was having in translating *Fin de partie (Endgame)* into English. The line Clov addresses to Hamm, 'Il n'y a plus de roues de bicyclette', was a particular problem. In French, Beckett contended, the line conveyed the meaning that bicycle wheels as a category had ceased to exist, that there were no more bicycle wheels in the world. The English equivalent, however, 'There are no more bicycle wheels', meant simply that there were no more bicycle wheels available, that no bicycle wheels could be found in the place where they happened to be. A world of difference is embedded here beneath apparent similarity. Just as the Eskimos have more than twenty words for snow (a frequently cited example), which means they are able to experience snow in ways far more nuanced and elaborate than we are – literally to see things we cannot see – the French live inside their language in ways that are somewhat at odds with the way we live inside English. There is no judgment of any kind attached to this remark. If bad French poetry tends to drift off into almost mechanical abstractions, bad English and American poetry has tended to be too earthbound and leaden, sinking into triviality and inconsequence. Between the two bads there is probably little to choose from. But it is helpful to remember that a good French poem is not necessarily the same thing as a good English poem.

The French have had their Academy for more than three hundred years. It is an institution that at once expresses and helps to perpetuate a notion of literature far more grandiose than anything we have ever known in England or America. As an official point of view, it has had the effect of removing the literary from the realm of the everyday, whereas English and American writers have generally been more at home in the flux of the quotidian. But because they have an established tradition to react against, French poets – paradoxically – have tended to be more rebellious than their British and American counterparts. The pressures of conformity have had the net result of producing a vigorous anti-tradition, which in many ways has actually usurped the established tradition as the major current in French literature. Beginning with Villon and Rabelais, continuing on through Rousseau, Baudelaire, Rimbaud, and the cult of the *poète maudit*, and then on into the twentieth century with Apollinaire, the Dada movement and the Surrealists, the French have systematically and defiantly attacked the accepted notions of their own culture – primarily because they have been secure in their knowledge that this culture exists. The lessons of this anti-tradition have been so thoroughly assimilated that today they are more or less taken for granted.

By contrast, the great interest shown by Pound and Eliot in French poetry (and, in Pound's case, the poetry of other languages as well) can be read not so much as an attack on Anglo-American culture as an effort to create a tradition, to manufacture a past that would somehow fill the vacuum of American newness. The impulse was essentially conservative in nature. With Pound, it degenerated into Fascist rantings; with Eliot, into Anglican pieties and an obsession with the notion of Culture. It would be wrong, however, to set up a simple dichotomy between radicalism and conservatism, and to put all things French in the first category and all things English and American in the second. The most subversive and innovative elements of our literature have frequently surfaced in the unlikeliest places and have then been absorbed into the culture at large. Nursery rhymes, which form an essential part of every English-speaking child's early education, do not exist as such in France. Nor do the great works of Victorian children's literature (Lewis Carroll, George Macdonald) have any equivalent in French. As for America, it has always had its own, homegrown Dada spirit, which has continued to exist as a natural force, without any need of manifestoes or theoretical foundations. The films of Buster Keaton and W. C. Fields, the skits of Ring Lardner, the drawings of Rube Goldberg surely match the corrosive exuberance of anything done in France during the same period. As Man Ray (a native American) wrote to Tristan Tzara from New York in 1921 about spreading the Dada movement to America: 'Cher Tzara – Dada cannot live in New York. All New York is Dada, and will not tolerate a rival ... '

Nor should one assume that twentieth-century French poetry is sitting out there as a convenient, self-contained entity. Far from being a unified body of work that resides neatly within the borders of France, French poetry of this century is various, tumultuous and contradictory. There is no typical case – only a horde of exceptions. For the fact is, a great number of the most original and influential poets were either born in other countries or spent a substantial part of their lives abroad. Apollinaire was born in Rome of mixed Polish and Italian parentage; Milosz was Lithuanian; Segalen spent his most productive years in China; Cendrars was born in Switzerland, composed his first major poem in New York, and until he was over fifty rarely stayed in France long enough to collect his mail; Saint-John Perse was born in Guadeloupe, worked for many years in Asia as a diplomat and lived almost exclusively in Washington,

D.C. from 1941 until his death in 1975; Supervielle was from Uruguay and for most of his life divided his time between Montevideo and Paris; Tzara was born in Rumania and came to Paris by way of the Dada adventures at the Cabaret Voltaire in Zurich, where he frequently played chess with Lenin; Jabès was born in Cairo and lived in Egypt until he was forty-five; Césaire is from Martinique; du Bouchet is part American and was educated at Amherst and Harvard; and nearly all the younger poets in this book have stayed for extended periods in either England or America. The stereotypical view of the French poet as a creature of Paris, as a xenophobic purveyor of French values, simply does not hold. The more intimately one becomes involved with the work of these poets, the more reluctant one becomes to make any generalizations about them. In the end, the only thing that can be said with any certainty is that they all write in French.

An anthology, therefore, is a kind of trap, tending to thwart our access to the poems even as it makes them available to us. By gathering the work of so many poets in one volume, the temptation is to consider the poets as a group, to drown them as individuals in the great pot of literature. Thus, even before it is read, the anthology becomes a kind of cultural dinner, a smattering of national dishes served up on a platter for popular consumption, as if to say, 'Here is French poetry. Eat it. It's good for you.' To approach poetry in that way is to miss the point entirely – for it allows one to avoid looking squarely at the poem on the page. And that, after all, is the reader's primary obligation. One must resist the notion of treating an anthology as the last word on its subject. It is no more than a first word, a threshold opening on to a new space.

3

In the end you are weary of this ancient world.
                        Guillaume Apollinaire

The logical place to begin this book is with Apollinaire. Although he is neither the first-born of the poets included nor the first to have written in a consciously modern idiom, he, more than any other artist of his time, seems to embody the aesthetic aspirations of the early part of the century. In his poetry, which ranges from graceful love lyrics to bold experiments, from rhyme to free verse to 'shape' poems, he manifests a new sensibility, at once indebted to the forms of the past and enthusiastically at home in the world of automobiles, airplanes and movies. As the tireless promoter of the Cubist painters, he was the figure around whom many of the best artists and writers gathered, and poets such as Jacob, Cendrars and Reverdy formed an important part of his circle. The work of these three, along with Apollinaire's, has frequently been described as Cubist. While there are vast differences among them, both in methods and tone, they nevertheless share a certain point of view, especially in the epistemological foundations of the work. Simultaneity, juxtaposition, an acute feeling for the jaggedness of the real – these are traits to be found in all four, and each exploits them to different poetic ends.

Cendrars, at once more abrasive and voluptuous than Apollinaire, observed that 'everything around me moves,' and his work oscillates between the two solutions implicit in this statement: on the one hand, the ebullient jangle of sensations in works such as *Nineteen Elastic Poems*, and on the other the snapshot realism of his travel poems (originally entitled *Kodak*, but changed under pressure from the film company of the same name, to *Documentaires*) – as if each of these poems was the record of a single moment, lasting no longer than it takes to click the shutter of a camera. With Jacob, whose most enduring work is contained in his 1917 collection of prose poems, *The Dice Cup*, the impulse is toward an anti-lyrical comedy. His language is continually erupting into playfulness (puns, parody, satire) and takes its greatest delight in unmasking the deceptions of appearances: Nothing is ever what it seems to be, everything is subject to metamorphosis, and change always occurs unexpectedly, with lightning swiftness.

Reverdy, by contrast, uses many of these same principles, but with far more somber objectives. Here an accumulation of fragments is synthesized into an entirely new approach to the poetic image. 'The image is a pure creation of the mind,' wrote Reverdy in 1918. 'It cannot be born from a comparison but from a juxtaposition of two more or less distant realities. The more the relationship between the two juxtaposed realities is both distant and true, the stronger the image will be – the greater its emotional power and poetic reality.' Reverdy's strange landscapes, which combine an intense inwardness with a proliferation of sensual data, bear in them the signs of a continual search for an impossible totality. Almost mystical in their effect, his poems are nevertheless anchored in the minutiae of the everyday world; in their quiet, at times monotone music, the poet seems to evaporate, to vanish into the haunted country he has created. The result is at once beautiful and disquieting – as if Reverdy had emptied the space of the poem in order to let the reader inhabit it.

A similar atmosphere is sometimes produced by the prose poems of Fargue, whose work predates that of any other poet included here. Fargue is the supreme modern poet of Paris, and fully half his writings are about the city itself. In his delicate, lyrical configurations of memory and perception, which retain an echo of their Symbolist predecessors, there is an attentiveness to detail combined with a rigorous subjectivity that transforms the city into an immense interior landscape. The poem of witness is at the same time a poem of remembrance, as if, in the solitary act of seeing, the world were reflected back to its solitary source and then, once more, reflected outward as vision. With Larbaud, a close friend of Fargue's, one also finds a hint of the late nineteenth century. A. O. Barnabooth, the supposed author of Larbaud's finest book of poems (in the first edition of 1908 Larbaud's name was intentionally left off the title page), is a rich South American of twenty-four, a naturalized citizen of New York, an orphan, a world traveler, a highly sensitive and melancholy young man – a more sympathetic and humorous version of the traditional dandy hero. As Larbaud later explained, he wanted to invent a poet 'sensitive to the diversity of races, people, and countries; who could find the exotic everywhere . . . ; witty and "international," one, in a word, capable of writing like Whitman but in a light vein, and of supplying that note of comic, joyous irresponsibility which is lacking in Whitman.' As in the poems of Apollinaire and Cendrars, Larbaud-Barnabooth expresses an almost euphoric delight in the sensations of travel: 'I experienced for the first time all the joy of living / In a compartment of the Nord-Express . . . ' Of Barnabooth André Gide wrote: 'I love his haste, his cynicism, his gluttony. These poems, dated from here and there, and everywhere, are as thirst-making as a wine list . . . In this particular book, each picture of sensation, no matter how correct or dubious it may be, is made valid by the speed with which it is supplanted.'

The work of Saint-John Perse also bears a definite resemblance to that of Whitman – both in the nature of his stanza and in the rolling, cumulative force of his long syntactic breaths. If Larbaud in some sense domesticates Whitman, Saint-John Perse carries him beyond universalism into a quest for great cosmic harmonies. The voice of the poet is mythical in its scope, as if, with its thunderous and sumptuous rhetoric, it had come into being for the sole purpose of conquering the world. Unlike most of the poets of his generation, who made their peace with temporality and used the notion of change as the premise of their work, Saint-John Perse's poems are quickened by an almost Platonic urge to seek out the eternal. In this respect, Milosz also stands to the side of his contemporaries. A student of the mystics and the alchemists, Milosz combines Catholicism and cabalism with what Kenneth Rexroth has described as 'apocalyptic sensualism', and his work draws much of its inspiration from numerological treatment of names, transpositions of letters, anagrammatic and acronymic combinations, and other linguistic practices of the occult. But, as with the poems of Yeats, the poetry itself transcends the restrictions of its sources, displaying, as John Peck has commented, 'an obsessive range of feeling, in which personal melancholy is also melancholy for a crepuscular era, that long hour before first light "when the shadows decompose".'

Another poet who resists categorization is Segalen. Like Larbaud, who wrote his poems through an invented persona; like Pound, whose translations stand curiously among his best and most personal works, Segalen carried this impulse toward self-effacement one step further and wrote behind the mask of another culture. The poems to be found in *Stèles* are neither translations nor imitations, but French poems written by a French poet *as if he were Chinese*. There is no attempt to deceive on Segalen's part; he never pretended these poems were anything other than original works. What at first reading might appear to be a kind of literary exoticism on closer scrutiny holds up as a poetry of solid, universal interest. By freeing himself from the limitations of his own culture, by circumventing his own historical moment, Segalen was able to explore a much wider territory – to discover, in some sense, that part of himself that was a poet.

In many ways, the case of Jouve is no less unusual. A follower of the Symbolists as a young man, Jouve published a number of books of poetry between 1912 and 1923. What he described as a 'moral, spiritual, and aesthetic crisis' in 1924 led him to break with all his early work, which he never allowed to be republished. Over the next forty years he produced a voluminous body of writing – his collected poems run well over a thousand pages. Deeply Christian in outlook, Jouve is primarily concerned with the question of sexuality, both as transgression and as creative force – 'the beautiful power of human eroticism' – and his poetry is the first in France to have made use of the methods of Freudian psychoanalysis. It is a poetry without predecessors and without followers. If his work was somewhat forgotten during the period dominated by the Surrealists – which meant that recognition of Jouve's achievement was delayed for almost a generation – he is now widely considered to be one of the major poets of the half-century.

Supervielle was also influenced by the Symbolists as a young man, and of all the poets of his generation he is perhaps the most purely lyrical. A poet of space, of the natural world, Supervielle writes from a position of supreme innocence. 'To dream is to forget the materiality of one's body,' he wrote in 1951, 'and to confuse to some degree the outer and the inner world ... People are sometimes surprised over my marvelling at the world. This arises as much from the permanency of my dreams as from my bad memory. Both lead me from surprise to surprise, and force me to be amazed at everything.'

It is this sense of amazement, perhaps, that best describes the work of these first eleven poets, all of whom began writing before World War I. The poets of the next generation, however, who came of age during the war itself, were denied the possibility of such innocent optimism. The war was not simply a conflict between armies but a profound crisis of values that transformed European consciousness, and the younger poets, while having absorbed the lessons of Apollinaire and his contemporaries, were compelled to respond to this crisis in ways that were without precedent. As Hugo Ball, one of the founders of Dada, noted in his diary in 1917: 'A thousand-year-old culture disintegrates. There are no columns and no supports, no foundations anymore – they have all been blown up ... The meaning of the world has disappeared.'

The Dada movement, which began in Zurich in 1916, was the most radical response to this sense of spiritual collapse. In the face of a discredited culture, the Dadaists challenged every assumption and ridiculed every belief of that culture. As artists, they attacked the notion of art itself, transforming their rage into a kind of subversive doubt, filled with caustic humour and willful self-contradiction. 'The true Dadaists are against Dada,' wrote Tzara in one of his manifestoes. The point was never to take anything at face value and never to take anything too seriously – especially oneself. The Socratic ironies of Marcel Duchamp's art are perhaps the purest expression of this attitude. In the realm of poetry, Tzara was no less sly or rambunctious. This is his recipe for writing a Dada poem: 'Take a newspaper. Take a pair of scissors. Select an article as long as you want your poem to be. Cut out the article. Then carefully cut out each of the words that form this article and put them in a bag. Shake gently. Then take out each scrap, one after the other. Conscientiously copy them in the order they left the bag. The poem will resemble you. And there you are, an infinitely original writer, with a charming sensibility, beyond the understanding of the vulgar.' If this is a poetry of chance, it should not be confused with the aesthetics of aleatory composition. Tzara's proposed method is an assault on the sanctity of Poetry, and it does not attempt to elevate itself to the status of an artistic ideal. Its function is purely negative. This is anti-art in its earliest incarnation, the 'anti-philosophy of spontaneous acrobatics.'

Tzara moved to Paris in 1919, introducing Dada to the French scene. Breton, Aragon, Éluard and Soupault all became participants in the movement. Inevitably, it did not last more than a few years. An art of total negation cannot survive, for its destructiveness must ultimately include itself. It was by drawing on the ideas and attitudes of Dada, however, that Surrealism became possible. 'Surrealism is pure psychic automatism,' Breton wrote in his first manifesto of 1924, 'whose intention is to express, verbally, in writing, or by other means, the real process of thought and thought's dictation, in the absence of all control exercised by reason and outside all aesthetic or moral preoccupations. Surrealism rests on the belief in the superior reality of certain previously neglected forms of association; in the omnipotence of dream, and in the disinterested play of thought.'

Like Dada, Surrealism did not offer itself as an aesthetic movement. Equating Rimbaud's cry to change life with Marx's injunction to change the world, the Surrealists sought to push poetry, in Walter Benjamin's phrase, 'to the utmost limits of possibility'. The attempt was to demystify art, to blur the distinctions between life and art, and to use the methods of art to explore the possibilities of human freedom. To quote Walter Benjamin again, from his prescient essay on the Surrealists published in 1929: 'Since Bakunin, Europe has lacked a radical concept of freedom. The Surrealists have one. They are the first to liquidate the liberal-moral-humanistic ideal of freedom, because they are convinced that "freedom, which on this earth can only be bought with a thousand of the hardest sacrifices, must be enjoyed unrestrictedly in its fullness, without any kind of programmatic calculation, as long as it lasts." ' For this reason, Surrealism associated itself closely with the politics of revolution (one of its magazines was even entitled *Surrealism in the Service of the Revolution*), flirting continually with the Communist Party and playing the role of fellow traveler during the era of the Popular Front – although refusing to submerge its identity in that of pure politics. Constant disputes over principles marked the history of the Surrealists, with Breton holding the middle ground between the activist and aesthetic wings of the group, frequently shifting positions in an effort to maintain a consistent program for Surrealism. Of all the poets associated with the movement, only Péret remained faithful to Breton over the long term. Soupault, by nature averse to the notion of literary movements, lost interest by 1927. Both Artaud and Desnos were excommunicated in 1929 – Artaud for opposing Surrealism's interest in politics and Desnos for supposedly compromising his integrity by working as a journalist. Aragon, Tzara and Éluard all joined the Communist Party in the thirties. Queneau and Prévert parted amicably after a brief association. Daumal, whose work was recognized by Breton as sharing the preoccupations of the Surrealists, declined an invitation to join the group. Char, ten or twelve years younger than most of the original members, was an early adherent but later broke with the movement and went on to do his best work during and after the war. Ponge's connection was peripheral, and Michaux, in some sense the most Surrealist of all French poets, never had anything to do with the group.

This same confusion exists when one examines the work of these poets. If 'pure psychic automatism' is the under-lying principle of Surrealist composition, only Péret seems to have stuck to it rigorously in the writing of his poems. Interestingly, his work is the least resonant of all the Sur-realists – notable more for its comic effects than for any uncovering of the 'convulsive beauty' that Breton envis-aged as the goal of Surrealist writing. Even in Breton's poetry, with its abrupt shifts and unexpected associations, there is an undercurrent of consistent rhetoric that makes the poems cohere as densely reasoned objects of thought. With Tzara as well, automatism serves almost as a rhetori-cal device. It is a method of discovery, not an end in itself. In his best work – especially the long, multifaceted *Approxi-mate Man* – a torrent of images organizes itself into a nearly systematic argument by means of repetition and variation, propelling itself forward in the manner of a musical compo-sition.

Soupault, on the other hand, is clearly a conscious crafts-man. While limited in range, his poetry displays a charm and a humility absent in the work of the other Surrealists. He is a poet of intimacy and pathos, at times strangely reminiscent of Verlaine, and if his poems have none of the flamboyance to be found in Tzara and Breton, they are more immediately accessible, more purely lyrical. By the same token, Desnos is a poet of plain speech, whose work often achieves a stunning lyrical intensity. His output extends from early experiments with language (dexterous, often dazzling exercises in word play) to free-verse love poems of great poignancy to longer, narrative poems and works in traditional forms. In an essay published just one year before his death, Desnos described his work as an effort 'to fuse popular language, even the most colloquial, with an inexpressible "atmosphere"; with a vital use of imagery, so as to annex for ourselves those domains which ... remain incompatible with the fiendish, plaguing poetic dignity which endlessly oozes from tongues ... '

With Éluard, arguably the greatest of the Surrealist poets, the love poem is accorded metaphysical status. His language, as limpid as anything to be found in Ronsard, is built on syntactic structures of extreme simplicity. Éluard uses the idea of love in his work to mirror the poetic process itself – as a way both to escape the world and to understand it. It is that irrational part of man which weds the inner to the outer, rooted in the physical and yet transcending matter, creating that uniquely human place in which man can discover his freedom. These same themes are present in Éluard's later work, particularly the poems written during the German Occupation, in which this notion of freedom is carried from the realm of the individual to that of an entire people.

If Éluard's work can be read as a continuous whole, Aragon's career as a poet divides into two distinct periods. Perhaps the most militant and provocative of the French Dadaists, he also played a leading role in the development of Surrealism and, after Breton, was the group's most active theorist. Attacked by Breton in the early thirties for the increasingly propagandist tone of his poetry, Aragon withdrew from the movement and joined the Communist Party. It was not until the war that he returned to the writing of poetry – and in a manner that bears almost no relation to his earlier work. His Resistance poems brought him national fame, and they are distinguished by their force and eloquence, but in their methods they are highly traditional, composed for the most part in alexandrines and rhyming stanzas.

Although Artaud was an early participant in Surrealism (for a time he even headed The Central Bureau for Surrealist Research) and although a number of his most important works were written during that period, he is a writer who stands so defiantly outside the traditional norms of literature that it is useless to label his work in any way. Properly speaking, Artaud is not a poet at all, and yet he has probably had a greater influence on the poets who came after him than any other writer of his generation. 'Where others present their works,' he wrote, 'I claim to do no more than show my mind.' His aim as a writer was never to create aesthetic objects – works that could be detached from their creator – but to record the state of mental and physical struggle in which 'words rot at the unconscious summons of the brain.' There is no division in Artaud between life and writing – and life not in the sense of biography, of external events, but life as it is lived in the intimacy of the body, of the blood that flows through one's veins. As such, Artaud is a kind of Ur-poet, whose work describes the process of thought and feeling before the advent of language, before the possibility of speech. It is at once a cry of suffering and a challenge to all our assumptions about the purpose of literature.

In a totally different way from Artaud, Ponge also commands a unique place among the writers of his generation. He is a writer of supremely classical values, and his work – most of it has been written in prose – is pristine in its clarity, highly sensitive to nuance and the etymological origins of words, which Ponge has described as the 'semantical thickness' of language. Ponge has invented a new kind of writing, a poetry of the object that is at the same time a method of contemplation. Minutely detailed in its descriptions, and everywhere infused with a fine ironic humor, his work proceeds as though the object being examined did not exist as a word. The primary act of the poet, therefore, becomes the act of seeing, as if no one had ever seen the thing before, so that the object might have 'the good fortune to be born into words.'

Like Ponge, who has frequently resisted the efforts of critics to classify him as a poet, Michaux is a writer whose work escapes the strictures of genre. Floating freely between prose and verse, his texts have a spontaneous, almost haphazard quality that sets them against the pretensions and platitudes of high art. No French writer has ever given greater rein to the play of his imagination. Much of his best writing is set in imaginary countries and reads as a bizarre kind of anthropology of inner states. Although often compared to Kafka, Michaux does not resemble the author of Kafka's novels and stories so much as the Kafka of the notebooks and parables. As with Artaud, there is an urgency of process in Michaux's writing, a sense of personal risk and necessity in the act of composition. In an early statement about his poetry he declared: 'I write with transport and for myself. a) sometimes to liberate myself from an intolerable tension or from a no less painful abandonment. b) sometimes for an imaginary companion, for a kind of alter ego whom I would honestly like to keep up-to-date on an extraordinary transition in me or in the world, which I, ordinarily forgetful, all at once believe I rediscover in, so to speak, its virginity. c) deliberately to shake the congealed and established, to invent ... Readers trouble me. I write, if you like, for the unknown reader.'

An equal independence of approach is present in Daumal, a serious student of Eastern religions, whose poems deal obsessively with the rift between spiritual and physical life. 'The Absurd is the purest and most basic form of metaphysical existence,' he wrote, and in his dense, visionary work, the illusions of appearance fall away only to be transformed into further illusions. 'The poems are haunted by a ... consciousness of impending death,' Michael Benedikt has commented, 'seen as the poet's long-lost "double"; and also by a personification of death as a sort of sinister mother, an exacting being avaricious in her search for beings to extinguish – but only so as to place upon them perversely the burden of further metamorphoses.'

Daumal is considered one of the chief precursors of the 'College of Pataphysics,' a mock-secret literary organization inspired by Alfred Jarry that included both Queneau and Prévert among its members. Humor is the guiding principle in the work of these two poets. With Queneau, it is a linguistic humor, based on intricate word plays, parody, feigned stupidity and slang. In his well-known prose work of 1947, for example, *Exercices de style*, the same mundane event is given in ninety-nine different versions, each one written in a different style, each one presented from a different point of view. In discussing Queneau in *Writing Degree Zero*, Roland Barthes describes this style as 'white writing' – in which literature, for the first time, has openly become a problem and question of language. If Queneau is an intellectual poet, Prévert, who also adheres closely to the patterns of ordinary speech in his work, is without question a popular poet – even a populist poet. Since World War II, no one has had a wider audience in France, and many of Prévert's works have been turned into highly successful songs. Anticlerical, antimilitaristic, rebellious in political attitude and extolling a rather sentimentalized form of love between man and woman, Prévert represents one of the more felicitous marriages between poetry and mass culture, and beyond the charm of his work, it is valuable as an indicator of popular French taste.

Although Surrealism continues to exist as a literary movement, the period of its greatest influence and most important creations came to an end by the beginning of World War II. Of the second-generation Surrealists – or those poets who found inspiration in its methods – Césaire stands out as the most notable example. One of the first black writers to be recognized in France, founder of the *négritude* movement – which asserts the uniqueness and dignity of black culture and consciousness – Césaire, a native of Martinique, was championed by Breton, who discovered his work in the late thirties. As the South African poet Mazisi Kunene has written about Césaire: 'Surrealism was for him a logical instrument with which to smash the restrictive forms of language which sanctified rationalized bourgeois values. The breaking up of language patterns coincided with his own desire to smash colonialism and all oppressive forms.' More vividly perhaps than in the work of the Surrealists of France, Césaire's poetry embodies the twin aspirations of political and aesthetic revolution, and in such a way that they are inseparably joined.

For many of the poets who began writing in the thirties, however, Surrealism was never a temptation. Follain, for example, whose work has proved to be particularly amenable to American taste (of all recent French poets, he is the one who has been most frequently translated), is a poet of the everyday, and in his short, exquisitely crafted works one finds an examination of the object no less serious and challenging than Ponge's. At the same time, Follain is largely a poet of memory ('In the fields / of his eternal childhood / the poet wanders / wanting to forget nothing'), and his evocations of the world as seen through a child's eyes bear within them a shimmering, epiphanic quality of psychological truth. A similar kind of realism and attention to surface detail is also to be found in Guillevic. Materialist in his approach to the world, unrhetorical in his methods, Guillevic has also created a world of objects – but one in which the object is nevertheless problematical, a reality to be penetrated, to be striven for, but which is not necessarily given. Frénaud, on the other hand, although often grouped together with Follain and Guillevic, is a far more romantic poet than his two contemporaries. Effusive in his language, metaphysical in his concerns, he has been compared at times to the Existentialists in his insistence that man's world is a creation of man himself. Despairing of certainty (*There Is No Paradise*, reads the title of one of his collections), Frénaud's work draws its force not so much from a recognition of the absurd as from the attempt to find a basis for positive values within the absurd itself.

If World War I was the crucial event that marked the poetry of the twenties and thirties, World War II was no less decisive in determining the kind of poetry written in France during the late forties and fifties. The military defeat of 1940 and the Nazi Occupation that followed were among the darkest moments in French history. The country had been devastated both emotionally and economically. In the context of this disarray, the mature poetry of René Char came as a revelation. Aphoristic, fragmented, closely allied to the thought of Heraclitus and the pre-Socratics, Char's poetry is at once a lyrical summoning of natural correspondences and a meditation on the poetic process itself. Austere in its settings (for the most part the landscape is that of Char's native Provence) and roughly textured in its language, this is a poetry that does not attempt to record or evoke feelings so much as it seeks to embody the ongoing struggle of words to ground themselves in the world. Char writes from a position of deep existential commitment (he was an important field leader in the Resistance), and his work is permeated with a sense of new beginnings, of a necessary search to rescue life from the ruins.

The best poets of the immediate postwar generation share many of these same preoccupations. Bonnefoy, du Bouchet, Jaccottet, Giroux and Dupin, all born within four years of each other, manifest in their work a vigilant hermeticism that is characterized by a consciously reduced range of imagery, great syntactical inventiveness and a refusal to ask anything but essential questions. Bonnefoy, the most classical and philosophically oriented of the five, has largely been concerned in his work with tracking the reality that haunts 'the abyss of concealed appearances.' 'Poetry does not interest itself in the shape of the world itself,' he once remarked, 'but in the world that this universe will become. Poetry speaks only of presences – or absences.' Du Bouchet, by contrast, is a poet who shuns every temptation toward abstraction. His work, which is perhaps the most radical adventure in recent French poetry, is based on a rigorous attentiveness to phenomenological detail. Stripped of metaphor, almost devoid of imagery, and generated by a language of abrupt, paratactic brevity, his poems move through an almost barren landscape, a speaking 'I' continually in search of itself. A du Bouchet page is the mirror of this journey, each one dominated by white space, the few words present as if emerging from a silence that will inevitably claim them again.

Of these poets, it is undoubtedly Dupin whose work holds the greatest verbal richness. Tightly sprung, calling upon an imagery that seethes with hidden violence, his poems are dazzling in both their energy and their anguish. 'In this infinite unanimous dissonance,' he writes, in a poem entitled 'Lichens,' 'each ear of corn, each drop of blood, speaks its language and goes its way. The torch,

which lights the abyss, which seals it up, is itself an abyss.'
Far gentler in approach are both Jaccottet and Giroux. Jaccottet's short nature poems, which in certain ways adhere
to the aesthetics of Imagism, have an Oriental stillness
about them that can flare at any moment into the brightness
of epiphany. 'For us living more and more surrounded by
intellectual schemas and masks,' Jaccottet has written, 'and
suffocating in the prison they erect around us, the poet's
eye is the battering ram that knocks down these walls and
gives back to us, if only for an instant, the real; and with
the real, a possibility of life.' Giroux, a poet of great lyrical
gifts, died prematurely in 1973 and published only one
book during his lifetime. The short poems in that volume
are quiet, deeply meditated works about the nature of
poetic reality, explorations of the space between the world
and words, and they have had a considerable impact on
the work of many of today's younger poets.

This hermeticism, however, is by no means present in
the work of all the poets of the postwar period. Dadelsen,
for example, is an effusive poet, monologic and varied in
tone, who frequently launches into slang. There have been
a number of distinguished Catholic poets in France during
the twentieth century (La Tour du Pin, Emmanuel, Jean-
Claude Renard and Mambrino are recent examples), but it
is perhaps Dadelsen, less well known than the others, who
in his tormented search for God best represents the limits
and perils of religious consciousness. Marteau, on the other
hand, draws much of his imagery from myth, and although
his preoccupations often overlap with those of, say, Bonnefoy or Dupin, his work is less self-reflective than theirs,
dwelling not so much on the struggles and paradoxes of
expression as on uncovering the presence of archetypal
forces in the world.

Of the new work that began to appear in the early sixties,

the books of Jabès are the most notable. Since 1963, when *The Book of Questions* was published, Jabès has brought out ten volumes in a remarkable series of works, prompting comments such as Jacques Derrida's statement that 'in the last ten years nothing has been written in France that does not have its precedent somewhere in the texts of Jabès.' Jabès, an Egyptian Jew who published a number of books of poetry in the forties and fifties, has emerged as a writer of the first rank with his more recent work – all of it written in France after his expulsion from Cairo during the Suez crisis. These books are almost impossible to define. Neither novels nor poems, neither essays nor plays, they are a combination of all these forms, a mosaic of fragments, aphorisms, dialogues, songs and commentaries that end-lessly move around the central question posed by each book: how to speak what cannot be spoken. The question is the Holocaust, but it is also the question of literature itself. By a startling leap of the imagination, Jabès treats them as one and the same: 'I have talked to you about the difficulty of being Jewish, which is the same as the diffi-culty of writing. For Judaism and writing are but the same waiting, the same hope, the same wearing out.'

This determination to carry poetry into uncharted terri-tory, to break down the standard distinctions between prose and verse, is perhaps the most striking characteristic of the younger generation of poets today. In Deguy, for example, poetry can be made from just about anything at all, and his work draws on a broad range of material: from the technical language of science to the abstractions of philo-sophy to elaborate play on linguistic constructions. In Rou-baud, the quest for new forms has led to books of highly intricate structures (one of his volumes, Σ, is based on the permutations of the Japanese game of go), and these invented shapes are exploited with great deftness, serving not as ends in themselves but as a means of ordering the fragments they encompass, of putting the various pieces in a larger context and investing them with a coherence they would not possess on their own.

Pleynet and Roche, two poets closely connected with the well-known review *Tel Quel*, have each carried the notion of antipoetry to a position of extreme combativeness. Pleynet's jocular, and at the same time deadly serious 'Ars Poetica' of 1964 is a good example of this attitude. 'I. ONE CANNOT KNOW HOW TO WRITE WITHOUT KNOWING WHY. II. THE AUTHOR OF THIS ARS POETICA DOES NOT KNOW HOW TO WRITE BUT HE WRITES. III. THE QUESTION "HOW TO WRITE" ANSWERS THE QUESTION "WHY WRITE" AND THE QUESTION "WHAT IS WRITING". IV. A QUESTION IS AN ANSWER.' Roche's approach is perhaps even more disruptive of conventional assumptions about literature. 'Poetry is inadmissible. Besides, it does not exist,' he has written. And elsewhere: ' . . . the logic of modern writing demands that one should take a vigorous hand in promoting the death agonies of [this] symbolist, outmoded ideology. Writing can only symbolize what it is in its functioning, in its 'society', within the frame of its utilization. It must stick to that.'

This is not to say, however, that short, lyric poems do not continue to be written in France. Delahaye and Denis, both still in their thirties, have created substantial bodies of work in this more familiar mode – mining a landscape that had first been mapped out by du Bouchet and Dupin. On the other hand, many of the younger poets, having absorbed and transmuted the questions raised by their predecessors, are now producing a kind of work that is both original and demanding in its insistence upon the textuality of the written word. Although there are significant differences among Albiach, Royet-Journoud, Daive, Hocquard and Veinstein, in one fundamental aspect of their work they share a common point of view. Their medium as writers is neither the individual poem nor even the sequence of poems, but the book. As Royet-Journoud stated in a recent interview: 'My books consist only of a single text, the genre of which cannot be defined. . . . It's a *book* that I write, and I feel that the notion of genre obscures the book as such.' This is as true of Daive's highly charged, psycho-erotic work, Hocquard's graceful and ironic narratives of memory, and Veinstein's minimal theaters of the creative process as it is of Royet-Journoud's obsessive 'detective stories' of language. Most strikingly, this approach to composition can be found in Albiach's 1971 volume, *État*, undoubtedly the major work to be published thus far by a member of this younger generation. As Keith Waldrop has written: 'The poem – it is a single piece – does not progress by images . . . or by plot. . . . The argument, if it were given, might include the following propositions: 1) everyday language is dependent on logic, but 2) in fiction, there is no necessity that any particular word should follow any other, so 3) it is possible at least to imagine a free choice, a syntax generated by desire. *État* is the "epic" . . . of this imagination. To state such an argument . . . would be to renounce the whole project. But what is presented is not a series of emotions . . . the poem is composed mindfully; and if Anne-Marie Albiach rejects rationality, she quite obviously writes with full intelligence . . .'

4

... with the conviction that, in the end, translating is madness.

Maurice Blanchot

As I was about to embark on the project of editing this anthology, a friend gave me a piece of valuable advice. Jonathan Griffin, who served as British cultural attaché in Paris after the war and has translated several books by De Gaulle as well as poets ranging from Rimbaud to Pessoa, has been around long enough to know more about such things than I do. Every anthology, he said, has two types of readers: the critics, who judge the book by what is *not* included in it, and the general readers, who read the book for what it actually contains. He advised me to keep this second group uppermost in my thoughts. The critics, after all, are in business to criticize, and they are familiar with the material anyway. The important thing to remember is that most people will be reading the majority of these poets for the first time. They are the ones who will get the most out of the anthology.

During the two years it has taken for me to put this book together, I have often reminded myself of these words. Frequently, however, it has been difficult to take them to heart, since I myself am all too aware of what has not been included. My original plan for the anthology was to represent the work of almost a hundred poets. In addition to more familiar kinds of writing, I had wanted to use a number of eccentric works, provide examples of concrete and sound poetry, include several collaborative poems and, in a few instances, offer variant translations when more than one good version of a poem was available. As work progressed, it became apparent that this would not be possible. I was faced with the unhappy situation of trying to fit an elephant into a cage designed for a fox. Reluctantly, I changed my approach to the book. If my choice was between offering a smattering of poems by many poets or substantial selections of work by a reduced number of poets, there did not seem to be much doubt that the second solution was wiser and more coherent. Instead of imagining everything I would like to see in the anthology, I tried to think of the poets it would be inconceivable *not* to include. In this way, I gradually whittled the list down to forty-eight. These were difficult decisions for me, and though I stand by my final selection, it is with regret for those I was not able to include.*

There are no doubt some who will also wonder about certain other exclusions. In order to keep the book focused on poetry of the twentieth century, I decided on a fixed cut-off point to determine where the anthology should begin. The crucial year for my purposes turned out to be 1876: any poet born before that year would not be considered. This allowed me, in good conscience, to forgo the problem posed by poets such as Valéry, Claudel, Jammes and Péguy, all of whom began writing in the late nineteenth century and went

---

*Among them are the following: Pierre Albert-Birot, Jean Cocteau, Raymond Roussel, Jean Arp, Francis Picabia, Arthur Cravan, Michel Leiris, Georges Bataille, Léopold Senghor, André Pieyre de Mandiargues, Jacques Audiberti, Jean Tardieu, Georges Schéhadé, Pierre Emmanuel, Joyce Mansour, Patrice de la Tour du Pin, René Guy Cadou, Henri Pichette, Christian Dotremont, Olivier Larronde, Henri Thomas, Jean Grosjean, Jean Tortel, Jean Laude, Pierre Torreilles, Jean-Claude Renard, Jean Joubert, Jacques Réda, Armen Lubin, Jean Pérol, Jude Stéfan, Marc Alyn, Jacqueline Risset, Michel Butor, Jean Pierre Faye, Alain Jouffroy, Georges Perros, Armand Robin, Boris Vian, Jean Mambrino, Lorand Gaspar, Georges Badin, Pierre Oster, Bernard Nöel, Claude Vigée, Joseph Gugliemi, Daniel Blanchard, Michel Couturier, Claude Esteban, Alain Sueid, Mathieu Bénézet.

on writing well into the twentieth. Although their work overlaps chronologically with many of the poets in the book, it seems to belong in spirit to an earlier time. By the same token, 1876 was a convenient date for allowing me to include certain poets whose work is essential to the project – Fargue, Jacob and Milosz in particular.

As for the English versions of the poems, I have used already existing translations whenever possible. My motive has been to underscore the involvement, over the past fifty years, of American and British poets in the work of their French counterparts, and since there is abundant material to choose from (some of it hidden away in old magazines and out-of-print books, some of it readily available), there seemed to be no need to begin my search elsewhere. My greatest pleasure in putting this book together has been in rescuing a number of superb translations from the obscurity of library shelves and microfilm rooms: Nancy Cunard's Aragon, John Dos Passos' Cendrars, Paul Bowles's Ponge, and the translations by Eugene and Maria Jolas (the editors of *transition*), to mention just a few. Also to be noted are the translations that previously existed only in manuscript. Paul Blackburn's translations of Apollinaire, for example, were discovered among his papers after his death, and are published here for the first time.

Only in cases where translations did not exist or where the available translations seemed inadequate did I commission fresh translations. In each of these instances (Richard Wilbur's version of Apollinaire's 'Le Pont Mirabeau', Lydia Davis's Fargue, Robert Kelly's Roubaud, Anselm Hollo's Dadelsen, Michael Palmer's Hocquard, Rosmarie Waldrop's Veinstein, Geoffrey Young's Aragon), I have tried to arrange the marriage with care. My aim was to bring together compatible poets – so that the translator would be able to exploit his particular strengths as a poet in rendering the original into English. The results of this matchmaking have been uniformly satisfying. Richard Wilbur's 'Mirabeau Bridge', for instance, strikes me as the first acceptable version of this important poem we have had in English, the only translation that comes close to recreating the subtle music of the original.

In general, I have followed no consistent policy about translation in making my choices. A few of the translations are hardly more than adaptations, although the vast majority are quite faithful to the originals. Translating poetry is at best an art of approximation, and there are no fixed rules to follow in deciding what works or does not. It is largely a matter of instinct, of ear, of common sense. Whenever I was faced with a choice between literalness and poetry, I did not hesitate to choose poetry. It seemed more important to me to give those readers who have no French a true sense of each poem *as a poem* than to strive for word-by-word exactness. The experience of a poem resides not only in each of its words, but in the interactions among those words – the music, the silences, the shapes – and if a reader is not somehow given the chance to enter the totality of that experience, he will remain cut off from the spirit of the original. It is for this reason, it seems to me, that poems should be translated by poets.

1981

Mallarmé's second child, Anatole, was born on July 16, 1871, when the poet was twenty-nine. The boy's arrival came at a moment of great financial stress and upheaval for the family. Mallarmé was in the process of negotiating a move from Avignon to Paris, and arrangements were not finally settled until late November, when the family installed itself at 29 rue de Moscou and Mallarmé began teaching at the Lycée Fontanes.

Mme Mallarmé's pregnancy had been extremely difficult, and in the first months of his life Anatole's health was so fragile that it seemed unlikely he would survive. 'I took him out for a walk on Thursday,' Mme Mallarmé wrote to her husband on October 7. 'It seemed to me that his fine little face was getting back some of its color . . . I left him very sad and discouraged, and even afraid that I would not see him anymore, but it's up to God now, since the doctor can't do anything more, but how sad to have so little hope of seeing this dear little person recover.'

Anatole's health, however, did improve. Two years later, in 1873, he reappears in the family correspondence in a series of letters from Germany, where Mallarmé's wife had taken the children to meet her father. 'The little one is like a blossoming flower,' she wrote to Mallarmé. 'Tole loves his grandfather, he does not want to leave him, and when he is gone, he looks for him all over the house.' In that same letter, nine-year-old Geneviève added: 'Anatole asks for papa all the time.' Two years later, on a second trip to Germany, there is further evidence of Anatole's robust health, for after receiving a letter from his wife, Mallarmé wrote proudly to his friend Cladel: 'Anatole showers stones and punches on the little Germans who come back to attack him in a group.' The following year, 1876, Mallarmé was absent from Paris for a few days and received this anecdote from his wife: 'Totol is a bad little boy. He did not notice you were gone the night you left; it was only when I put him to bed that he looked everywhere for you to say goodnight. Yesterday he did not ask for you, but this morning the poor little fellow looked all over the house for you; he even pulled back the covers on your bed, thinking he would find you there.' In August of that same year, during another of Mallarmé's brief absences from the family, Geneviève wrote to her father to thank him for sending her presents and then remarked: 'Tole wants you to bring him back a whale.'

Beyond these few references to Anatole in the Mallarmé family letters, there are several mentions of him in C. L. Lefèvre-Roujon's introduction to the *Correspondance inédite de Stephane Mallarmé et Henry Roujon* – in particular, three little incidents that give some idea of the boy's lively personality. In the first, a stranger saw Anatole attending to his father's boat and asked him, 'What is your boat called?' Anatole answered with great conviction, 'My boat isn't called anything. Do you give a name to a carriage?' On another occasion, Anatole was taking a walk through the Fountainebleau forest with Mallarmé. 'He loved the Fontainebleau forest and would often go there with Stéphane. . . . [One day], running down a path, he came upon a very pretty woman, politely stepped to the side, looked her over from top to bottom and, out of admiration, winked his eye at her, clicked his tongue, and then, this homage to beauty having been made, continued on his child's promenade.' Finally, Lefèvre-Roujon reports the following: one day Mme Mallarmé boarded a Paris bus with Anatole and put the child on her lap in order to economize on the extra fare. As the bus jolted along, Anatole fell into a kind of trance, watching a gray-haired priest beside him who was reading his breviary. He asked him sweetly: 'Monsieur l'abbée, would you allow me to kiss you?' The priest, surprised and touched, answered: 'But of course, my little friend.' Anatole leaned over and kissed him. Then, in the suavest voice possible, he commanded: 'And now, kiss mama!'

In the spring of 1879, several months before his eighth birthday, Anatole became seriously ill. The disease, diagnosed as child's rheumatism, was further complicated by an enlarged heart. The illness first attacked his feet and knees, and then, when the symptoms had apparently cleared up, his ankles, wrists, and shoulders. Mallarmé considered himself largely responsible for the child's suffering, feeling that he had given the boy 'bad blood' through a hereditary weakness. At the age of seventeen, he had suffered terribly from rheumatic pain, with high fevers and violent headaches, and throughout his life rheumatism would remain a chronic problem.

In April, Mallarmé went off to the country for a few days with Geneviève. His wife wrote: 'He's been a good boy, the poor little martyr, and from time to time asks me to dry his tears. He asks me often to tell little papa that he would like to write to him, but he can't move his little wrists.' Three days later, the pain had shifted from Anatole's hands to his legs, and he was able to write a few words: 'I think of you always. If you knew, my dear Little Father, how my knees hurt.'

Over the following months, things took a turn for the better. By August, the improvement had been considerable.

On the tenth, Mallarmé wrote to Robert de Montesquiou, a recently made friend who had formed a special attachment to Anatole, to thank him for sending the child a parrot:

> I believe that your delicious little animal ... has distracted the illness of our patient, who is now allowed to go to the country ... Have you heard from where you are ... all the cries of joy from our invalid, who never takes his eyes ... away from the marvelous princess held captive in her marvelous palace, who is called Sémiramas because of the stone gardens she seems to reflect? I like to think that this satisfaction of an old and improbable desire has had something to do with the struggle of the boy's health to come back; to say nothing ... of the secret influence of the precious stone that darts out continually from the cage's inhabitant on the child ... How charming and friendly you have been, you who are so busy with so much, during this recent time; and it is more than a pleasure for me to announce to you, before anyone else, that I feel all our worries will soon be over.

In this state of optimism, Anatole was taken by the family to Valvins in the country. After several days, however, his condition deteriorated drastically, and he nearly died. On August 22, Mallarmé wrote to his close friend Henry Roujon:

> I hardly dare to give any news because there are moments in this war between life and death that our poor little adored one is waging when I allow myself to hope, and repent of a too sad letter written the moment before, as of some messenger of bad tidings I myself have dispatched. I know nothing anymore and

see nothing anymore ... so much have I observed with conflicting emotions. The doctor, while continuing the Paris treatment, seems to act as though he were dealing with a condemned person who can only be comforted; and persists, when I follow him to the door, in not giving a glimmer of hope. The dear boy eats and sleeps a little; breathes. Everything his organs could do to fight the heart problem they have done; after another enormous attack, that is the benefit he draws from the country. But the disease, the terrible disease, seems to have set in irremediably. If you lift the blanket, you see a belly so swollen you can't look at it!

There it is. I do not speak to you for my pain; no matter where my thought tries to lead it, this pain recoils from seeing itself worsen! But what does suffering matter, even suffering like that: the horrible thing is ... the misfortune in itself that this little being might vanish ... I confess that it is too much for me; I cannot bring myself to face this idea.

When my wife looks at the darling, she seems to see a serious illness and nothing more; I must not rob her of the courage she has found to care for the child in this quietude. I am alone here then with the hatchet blow of the doctor's verdict.

A letter from Mallarmé to Montesquiou on September 9 offers further details:

Unfortunately, after several days [in the country], everything ... grew dark: we have been through the cruelest hours our darling invalid has caused us, for the symptoms we thought had disappeared forever have returned; they are taking hold now. The old improvements were a sham ... I am too tormented and too taken up with our poor little boy to do any-

thing literary, except to jot down a few rapid notes ...
Tole speaks of you, and even amuses himself in the
morning by fondly imitating your voice. The parrot,
whose auroral belly seems to catch fire with a whole
orient of spices, is looking right now at the forest with
one eye and at the bed with the other, like a thwarted
desire for an excursion by her little master.

By late September there had been no improvement, and
Mallarmé now centered his hopes on a return to Paris.
On the twenty-fifth, he wrote to his oldest friend, Henri
Cazalis:

> The evening before your beautiful present came, the
> poor darling, for the second time since his illness
> began, was nearly taken from us. Three successive
> fainting fits in the afternoon did not, thank heaven,
> carry him off ... The belly disturbs us, as filled with
> water as ever ... The country has given us everything
> we could ask of it, assuming it could give us anything,
> milk, air, and peaceful surroundings for the invalid.
> We have only one idea now, to leave for a consultation
> with Doctor Peter ... I tell myself it is impossible that
> a great medical specialist cannot take advantage of the
> forces nature opposes so generously to a terrible dis-
> ease ...

After the return to Paris, there are two further letters
about Anatole – both dated October 6. The first was to the
English writer John Payne:

> This is the reason for my long silence ... At Easter,
> already six hideous months ago, my son was attacked
> by rheumatism, which after a false convalescence has
> thrown itself on his poor heart with incredible vio-
> lence, and holds him between life and death. The poor

friend has twice almost been taken from us ... You
can judge of our pain, knowing how much I live inside
my family; then this child, so charming and exquisite,
had captivated me to the point that I still include him
in all my future projects and in my dearest dreams ...

The other letter was to Montesquiou.

Thanks to immense precautions, everything went well
[on the return to Paris] ... but the darling paid for it
with several bad days that drained his tiny energy. He
is prey to a horrible and inexplicable nervous cough
... it shakes him for a whole day and a whole night
... – Yes, I am quite beside myself, like someone on
whom a terrible and endless wind is blowing. All-
night vigils, contradictory emotions of hope and
sudden fear, have supplanted all thought of repose ...
My sick little boy smiles at you from his bed, like a
white flower remembering the vanished sun.

After writing these two letters, Mallarmé went to the
post office to mail them. Anatole died before his father
managed to return home.

The 202 fragments that follow belonged to Mme E. Bonniot,
the Mallarmé heir, and were deciphered, edited, and published in a scrupulously prepared volume by the literary
scholar and critic Jean-Pierre Richard in 1961. In the preface
to his book – which includes a lengthy study of the fragments – he describes his feelings on being handed the soft
red box that contained Mallarmé's notes. On the one hand:
exaltation. On the other hand: wariness. Although he was
deeply moved by the fragments, he was uncertain whether
publication was appropriate, given the intensely private
nature of the work. He concluded, however, that anything

that could enhance our understanding of Mallarmé would be valuable:

> And if these phrases are no more than sighs, that makes them all the more precious to us. It seemed to me that the very nakedness of these notes ... made their distribution desirable. It was useful in fact to prove once again to what extent the famous Mallar-méan serenity was based on the impulses of a very vivid sensibility, at times even quite close to frenzy and delirium ... Nor was it irrelevant to show, by means of a precise example, how this impersonality, this vaunted objectivity, was in reality connected to the most subjective upheavals of a life.

A close reading of the fragments will clearly show that they are no more than notes for a possible work: a long poem in four parts with a series of very specific themes. That Mallarmé projected such a work and then abandoned it is indicated in a memoir written by Geneviève that was published in a 1926 issue of the N.R.F.:

> In 1879, we had the immense sorrow of losing my little brother, an exquisite child of eight. I was quite young then, but the deep and silent pain I felt in my father made an unforgettable impression on me: 'Hugo,' he said, 'was happy to have been able to speak (about the death of his daughter); for me, it's impossible.'

As they stand now, the notes are a kind of ur-text, the raw data of the poetic process. Although they seem to resemble poems on the page, they should not be confused with poetry per se. Nevertheless, more than one hundred years after they were written, they are perhaps closer to what we today consider possible in poetry than at the time of their composition. For here we find a language of immediate contact, a syntax of abrupt, lightning shifts that still manages to maintain a sense, and in their brevity, the sparse presence of their words, we are given a rare and early example of isolated words able to span the enormous mental spaces that lie between them – as if intelligible links could be created by the brute force of each word or phrase, so densely charged that these tiny particles of language could somehow leap out of themselves and catch hold of the succeeding cliff-edge of thought.

Unlike Mallarmé's finished poems, these fragments have a startlingly unmediated quality. Faithful not to the demands of art but to the jostling movement of thought – and with a speed and precision that astonish – these notes seem to emerge from such an interior place, it is as though we could hear the crackling of the wires in Mallarmé's brain, experience each synapse of thought as a physical sensation. If these fragments cannot be read as a work of art, neither, I think, should they be treated simply as a scholarly appendage to Mallarmé's collected writings. For, in spite of everything, the Anatole notes do carry the force of poetry, and in the end they achieve a stunning wholeness. They are a work in their own right – but one that cannot be categorized, one that does not fit into any pre-existant literary form.

The subject matter of the fragments requires little comment. In general, Mallarmé's motivation seems to have been the following: feeling himself responsible for the disease that led to Anatole's death, for not giving his son a body strong enough to withstand the blows of life, he would take it upon himself to give the boy the one indomitable thing he was capable of giving: his thought. He would transmute Anatole into words and thereby prolong his life. He would, *literally*, resurrect him, since the work of building a tomb – a tomb of poetry – would obliterate the presence of death. For Mallarmé, death is the consciousness of death, not the physical act of dying. Because Anatole was too young to understand his fate (a theme that occurs repeatedly throughout the fragments), it was as though he had not yet died. He was still alive in his father, and it was only when Mallarmé himself died that the boy would die as well. This is one of the most moving accounts of a man trying to come to grips with modern death – that is to say, death without God, death without hope of salvation – and it reveals the secret meaning of Mallarmé's entire aesthetic: the elevation of art to the stature of religion. Here, however, the work could not be written. In this time of crisis, even art failed Mallarmé.

It strikes me that the effect of the Anatole fragments is quite close to the feeling created by Rembrandt's last portrait of his son, Titus. Bearing in mind the radiant and adoring series of canvasses the artist made of the boy throughout his childhood, it is almost impossible for us to look at that last painting: the dying Titus, barely twenty years old, his face so ravaged by disease that he looks like an old man. It is important to imagine what Rembrandt must have felt as he painted that portrait; to imagine him staring into the face of his dying son and being able to keep his hand steady enough to put what he saw onto the canvas. If fully imagined, the act becomes almost unthinkable.

In the natural order of things, fathers do not bury their sons. The death of a child is the ultimate horror of every parent, an outrage against all we believe we can expect of life, little though it is. For everything, at that point, is taken away from us. Unlike Ben Jonson, who could lament the fact of his fatherhood as an impediment to understanding that his son had reached 'the state he should envie', Mallarmé could find no support for himself, only an abyss, no consolation, except in the plan to write about his son – which, in the end, he could not bring himself to do. The work died along with Anatole. It is all the more moving to us, all the more important, for having been left unfinished.

1982

The first time I saw Philippe Petit was in 1971. I was in
Paris, walking down the Boulevard Montparnasse, when I
came upon a large circle of people standing silently on the
sidewalk. It seemed clear that something was happening
inside that circle, and I wanted to know what it was. I
elbowed my way past several onlookers, stood on my toes,
and caught sight of a smallish young man in the center.
Everything he wore was black: his shoes, his pants, his
shirt, even the battered silk top hat he wore on his head.
The hair jutting out from under the hat was a light red-
blond, and the face below it was so pale, so devoid of color,
that at first I thought he was in whiteface.

The young man juggled, rode a unicycle, performed little
magic tricks. He juggled rubber balls, wooden clubs, and
burning torches, both standing on the ground and sitting
on his one-wheeler, moving from one thing to the next
without interruption. To my surprise, he did all this in
silence. A chalk circle had been drawn on the sidewalk,
and scrupulously keeping any of the spectators from enter-
ing that space – with a persuasive mime's gesture – he
went through his performance with such ferocity and intelligence that it was impossible to stop watching.

Unlike other street performers, he did not play to the
crowd. Rather, it was somehow as though he had allowed
the audience to share in the workings of his thoughts, had
made us privy to some deep, inarticulate obsession within

him. Yet there was nothing overtly personal about what he did. Everything was revealed metaphorically, as if at one remove, through the medium of the performance. His juggling was precise and self-involved, like some conversation he was holding with himself. He elaborated the most complex combinations, intricate mathematical patterns, arabesques of nonsensical beauty, while at the same time keeping his gestures as simple as possible. Through it all, he managed to radiate a hypnotic charm, oscillating somewhere between demon and clown. No one said a word. It was as though his silence were a command for others to be silent as well. The crowd watched, and after the performance was over, everyone put money in the hat. I realized that I had never seen anything like it before.

The next time I saw Philippe Petit was several weeks later. It was late at night – perhaps one or two in the morning – and I was walking along a quai of the Seine not far from Nôtre-Dame. Suddenly, across the street, I spotted several young people moving quickly through the darkness. They were carrying ropes, cables, tools, and heavy satchels. Curious as ever, I kept pace with them from my side of the street and recognized one of them as the juggler from the Boulevard Montparnasse. I knew immediately that something was going to happen. But I could not begin to imagine what it was.

The next day, on the front page of the *International Herald Tribune,* I got my answer. A young man had strung a wire between the towers of Nôtre-Dame Cathedral and walked and juggled and danced on it for three hours, astounding the crowds of people below. No one knew how he had rigged up his wire nor how he had managed to elude the attention of the authorities. Upon returning to the ground, he had been arrested, charged with disturbing the peace and sundry other offenses. It was in this article that I first learned his name: Philippe Petit. There was not the slightest doubt in my mind that he and the juggler were the same person.

This Nôtre-Dame escapade made a deep impression on me, and I continued to think about it over the years that followed. Each time I walked past Nôtre-Dame, I kept seeing the photograph that had been published in the newspaper: an almost invisible wire stretched between the enormous towers of the cathedral, and there, right in the middle, as if suspended magically in space, the tiniest of human figures, a dot of life against the sky. It was impossible for me not to add this remembered image to the actual cathedral before my eyes, as if this old monument of Paris, built so long ago to the glory of God, had been transformed into something else. But what? It was difficult for me to say. Into something more human, perhaps. As though its stones now bore the mark of a man. And yet, there was no real mark. I had made the mark with my own mind, and it existed only in memory. And yet, the evidence was irrefutable: my perception of Paris had changed. I no longer saw it in the same way.

It is, of course, an extraordinary thing to walk on a wire so high off the ground. To see someone do this triggers an almost palpable excitement in us. In fact, given the necessary courage and skill, there are probably very few people who would not want to do it themselves. And yet, the art of high-wire walking has never been taken very seriously. Because wire walking generally takes place in the circus, it is automatically assigned marginal status. The circus, after all, is for children, and what do children know about art? We grown-ups have more important things to think about. There is the art of music, the art of painting, the art of sculpture, the art of poetry, the art of prose, the art of theater, the art of dancing, the art of cooking, the art of living. But the art of high-wire walking? The very term seems laughable. If people stop to think about the high-wire at all, they usually categorize it as some minor form of athletics.

There is, too, the problem of showmanship. I mean the crazy stunts, the vulgar self-promotion, the hunger for publicity that is everywhere around us. We live in an age when people seem willing to do anything for a little attention. And the public accepts this, granting notoriety or fame to anyone brave enough or foolish enough to make the effort. As a general rule, the more dangerous the stunt, the greater the recognition. Cross the ocean in a bathtub, vault forty burning barrels on a motorcycle, dive into the East River from the top of the Brooklyn Bridge, and you are sure to get your name in the newspapers, maybe even an interview on a talk show. The idiocy of these antics is obvious. I'd much rather spend my time watching my son ride his bicycle, training wheels and all.

Danger, however, is an inherent part of high-wire walking. When a man walks on a wire two inches off the ground, we do not respond in the same way as when he walks on a wire two hundred feet off the ground. But danger is only half of it. Unlike the stuntman, whose performance is calculated to emphasize every hair-raising risk, to keep his audience panting with dread and an almost sadistic anticipation of disaster, the good high-wire walker strives to make his audience forget the dangers, to lure it away from thoughts of death by the beauty of what he does on the wire itself. Working under the greatest possible constraints, on a stage no more than an inch across, the high-wire walker's job is to create a sensation of limitless freedom. Juggler, dancer, acrobat, he performs in the sky what other men are content to perform on the ground. The desire is at once far-fetched and perfectly natural, and the appeal of it, finally, is its utter uselessness. No art, it seems to me, so clearly emphasizes the deep aesthetic impulse inside us all. Each time we see a man walk on the wire, a part of us is up there with him. Unlike performances in the other arts, the experience of the high wire is direct, unmediated, simple, and it requires no explanation whatsoever. The art is the thing itself, a life in its most naked delineation. And if there is beauty in this, it is because of the beauty we feel inside ourselves.

There was another element of the Nôtre-Dame spectacle that moved me: the fact that it was clandestine. With the thoroughness of a bank robber preparing a heist, Philippe had gone about his business in silence. No press conferences, no publicity, no posters. The purity of it was impressive. For what could he possibly hope to gain? If the wire had snapped, if the installation had been faulty, he would have died. On the other hand, what did success bring? Certainly he did not earn any money from the venture. He did not even try to capitalize on his brief moment of glory. When all was said and done, the only tangible result was a short stay in a Paris jail.

Why did he do it, then? For no other reason, I believe, than to dazzle the world with what he could do. Having seen his stark and haunting juggling performance on the street, I sensed intuitively that his motives were not those of other men – not even those of other artists. With an ambition and an arrogance fit to the measure of the sky, and placing on himself the most stringent internal demands, he wanted, simply, to do what he was capable of doing.

After living in France for four years, I returned to New York in July of 1974. For a long time I had heard nothing about Philippe Petit, but the memory of what had happened in Paris was still fresh, a permanent part of my inner mythology. Then, just one month after my return, Philippe was in the news again – this time in New York, with his now-famous walk between the towers of the World Trade Center. It was good to know that Philippe was still dreaming his dreams, and it made me feel that I had chosen the right moment to come home. New York is a more generous city than Paris, and the people here responded enthusiastically to what he had done. As with the aftermath of the Nôtre-Dame adventure, however, Philippe kept faith with his vision. He did not try to cash in on his new celebrity; he managed to resist the honky-tonk temptations America is all too willing to offer. No books were published, no films were made, no entrepreneur took hold of him for packaging. The fact that the World Trade Center did not make him rich was almost as remarkable as the event itself. But the proof of this was there for all New Yorkers to see: Philippe continued to make his living by juggling in the streets.

The streets were his first theater, and he still takes his performances there as seriously as his work on the wire. It all started very early for him. Born into a middle-class French family in 1949, he taught himself magic at the age of six, juggling at the age of twelve, and high-wire walking a few years later. In the meantime, while immersing himself in such varied activities as horseback riding, rock-climbing, art, and carpentry, he managed to get himself expelled from nine schools. At sixteen, he began a period of incessant travels all over the world, performing as a street juggler in Western Europe, Russia, India, Australia, and the United States. 'I learned to live by my wits,' he has said of those years. 'I offered juggling shows everywhere, for everyone – traveling around like a troubadour with my old leather sack. I learned to escape the police on my unicycle. I got hungry like a wolf; I learned how to control my life.'

But it is on the high-wire that Philippe has concentrated

his most important ambitions. In 1973, just two years after the Nôtre-Dame walk, he did another renegade perform-ance in Sydney, Australia: stretching his wire between the northern pylons of the Harbour Bridge, the largest steel arch bridge in the world. Following the World Trade Center Walk in 1974, he crossed the Great Falls of Paterson, New Jersey, appeared on television for a walk between the spires of the Cathedral in Laon, France, and also crossed the Superdome in New Orleans before 80,000 people. This last performance took place just nine months after a forty-foot fall from an inclined wire, from which he suffered several broken ribs, a collapsed lung, a shattered hip, and a smashed pancreas.

Philippe has also worked in the circus. For one year he was a featured attraction with Ringling Brothers Barnum and Bailey, and from time to time he has served as a guest performer with The Big Apple Circus in New York. But the traditional circus has never been the right place for Philippe's talents, and he knows it. He is too solitary and unconventional an artist to fit comfortably into the stric-tures of the commercial big top. Far more important to him are his plans for the future: to walk across Niagara Falls; to walk from the top of the Sydney Opera House to the top of the Harbour Bridge – an inclined walk of more than half a mile. As he himself explains it: 'To talk about records or risks is to miss the point. All my life I have looked for the most amazing places to cross – mountains, waterfalls, buildings. And if the most beautiful walks also happen to be the longest or the most dangerous – that's fine. But I didn't look for that in the first place. What interests me is the performance, the show, the beautiful gesture.'

When I finally met Philippe in 1980, I realized that all my feelings about him had been correct. This was not a daredevil or a stuntman, but a singular artist who could talk about his work with intelligence and humor. As he said to me that day, he did not want people to think of him as just another 'dumb acrobat'. He talked about some of the things he had written – poems, narratives of his Nôtre-Dame and World Trade Center adventures, film scripts, a small book on high-wire walking – and I said that I would be interested in seeing them. Several days later, I received a bulky package of manuscripts in the mail. A covering note explained that these writings had been rejected by eighteen different publishers in France and America. I did not consider this to be an obstacle. I told Philippe that I would do all I could to find him a publisher and also promised to serve as translator if necessary. Given the pleasure I had received from his performances on the street and wire, it seemed the least I could do.

On the High Wire is in my opinion a remarkable book. Not only is it the first study of high-wire walking ever written, but it is also a personal testament. One learns from it both the art and the science of wire walking, the lyricism and the technical demands of the craft. At the same time, it should not be misconstrued as a 'how to' book or an instruction manual. High-wire walking cannot really be taught: it is something you learn by yourself. And certainly a book would be the last place to turn if you were truly serious about doing it.

The book, then, is a kind of parable, a spiritual journey in the form of a treatise. Through it all, one feels the presence of Philippe himself: it is his wire, his art, his personality that inform the entire discourse. No one else, finally, has a place in it. This is perhaps the most important lesson to be learned from the treatise: the high-wire is an art of solitude, a way of coming to grips with one's life in the darkest, most secret corner of the self. When read carefully, the book is transformed into the story of a quest, an exemplary tale of one man's search for perfection. As such, it has more to do with the inner life than the high-wire. It seems to me that anyone who has ever tried to do something well, anyone who has ever made personal sacrifices for an art or an idea, will have no trouble understanding what it is about.

Until two months ago, I had never seen Philippe perform on the high-wire outdoors. A performance or two in the circus, and of course films and photographs of his exploits, but no outdoor walk in the flesh. I finally got my chance during the recent inauguration ceremony at the Cathedral of Saint John the Divine in New York. After a hiatus of several decades, construction was about to begin again on the cathedral's tower. As a kind of homage to the wire walkers of the Middle Ages – the *joglar* from the period of the great French cathedrals – Philippe had conceived of the idea of stretching a steel cable from the top of a tall apartment building on Amsterdam Avenue to the top of the cathedral across the street – an inclined walk of several hundred yards. He would go from one end to the other and then present the Bishop of New York with a silver trowel, which would be used to lay the symbolic first stone of the tower.

The preliminary speeches lasted a long time. One after the other, dignitaries got up and spoke about the cathedral and the historic moment that was about to take place. Clergymen, city officials, former Secretary of State Cyrus Vance – all of them made speeches. A large crowd had gathered in the street, mostly school children and neighborhood people, and it was clear that the majority of them had come to see Philippe. As the speeches droned on, there was a good deal of talking and restlessness in the crowd. The late September weather was threatening: a raw, pale gray sky; the wind beginning to rise; rain clouds gathering in the distance. Everyone was impatient. If the speeches went on any longer, perhaps the walk would have to be canceled.

Fortunately, the weather held, and at last Philippe's turn came. The area below the cable had to be cleared of people, which meant that those who a moment before had held center stage were now pushed to the side with the rest of us. The democracy of it pleased me. By chance, I found myself standing shoulder to shoulder with Cyrus Vance on the steps of the cathedral. I, in my beat-up leather jacket, and he in his impeccable blue suit. But that didn't seem to matter. He was just as excited as I was. I realized later that at any other time I might have been tongue-tied to be standing next to such an important person. But none of that even occurred to me then. We talked about the high-wire and the dangers Philippe would have to face. He seemed to be genuinely in awe of the whole thing and kept looking up at the wire – as I did, as did the hundreds of children around us. It was then that I understood the most important aspect of the high-wire: it reduced us all to our common humanity. A Secretary of state, a poet, a child: we became equal in each other's eyes, and therefore a part of each other.

A brass band played a Renaissance fanfare from some invisible place behind the cathedral facade, and Philippe emerged from the roof of the building on the other side of the street. He was dressed in a white satin medieval costume, the silver trowel hanging from a sash at his side. He saluted the crowd with a graceful, bravura gesture, took hold of his balancing-pole firmly in his two hands, and began his slow ascent along the wire. Step by step, I felt myself walking up there with him, and gradually those heights seemed to become habitable, human, filled with happiness. He slid down to one knee and acknowledged the crowd again; he balanced on one foot; he moved deliberately and majestically, exuding confidence. Then, suddenly, he came to a spot on the wire far enough away from his starting-point that my eyes lost contact with all surrounding references: the apartment building, the street, the other people. He was almost directly overhead now, and as I leaned backward to take in the spectacle, I could see no more than the wire, Philippe, and the sky. There was nothing else. A white body against a nearly white sky, as if free. The purity of that image burned itself into my mind and is still there today, wholly present.

From beginning to end, I did not once think that he might fall. Risk, fear of death, catastrophe: these were not part of the performance. Philippe had assumed full responsibility for his own life, and I sensed that nothing could possibly shake that resolve. High-wire walking is not an art of death, but an art of life – and life lived to the very extreme of life. Which is to say, life that does not hide from death, but stares it straight in the face. Each time he sets foot on the wire, Philippe takes hold of that life and lives it in all its exhilarating immediacy, in all its joy.

May he live to be a hundred.

1982

III

Interviews

TRANSLATION

An Interview with Stephen Rodefer

STEPHEN RODEFER: *When did you begin doing translations?*
PAUL AUSTER: Back when I was nineteen or twenty years old, as an undergraduate at Columbia. They gave us various poems to read in French class – Baudelaire, Rimbaud, Verlaine – and I found them terribly exciting, even if I didn't always understand them. The foreignness was daunting to me – as though a work written in a foreign language was somehow not real – and it was only by trying to put them into English that I began to penetrate them. At that point, it was a strictly private activity for me, a method to help me understand what I was reading, and I had no thoughts about trying to publish what I did. I suppose you could say that I started doing translations because I was such a slow learner. I couldn't imagine a linguistic reality other than English, and I was driven by a need to appropriate these works, to make them part of my own world.

SR: *Were you writing poetry of your own at that time, too?*
PA: Yes. But like most young people, I had no idea what I was doing. One's ambitions at that stage are so enormous, but you don't necessarily have the tools to carry them out. It leads to frustration, a deep sense of your own inadequacy. I struggled along during those years to find my own way, and in the process I discovered that translation was an extremely helpful exercise. Pound recommends translation for young poets, and I think that shows great

understanding on his part. You have to begin slowly. Translation allows you to work on the nuts and bolts of your craft, to learn how to live intimately with words, to see more clearly what you are actually doing. That is the positive benefit, but there is also a negative one. Working on translations removes the pressure of composition. There is no need to be brilliant and original, no need to attempt things that you are finally not capable of doing. You learn how to feel more comfortable with yourself in the act of writing, and that is probably the most crucial thing for a young person. You submit yourself to someone else's work – someone who is necessarily more accomplished than you are – and you begin to read more profoundly and intelligently than you ever have before. Scholarly analysis of poetry serves an important function, but this kind of practical experience is irreplaceable. A young poet will learn more about how Rilke wrote sonnets by trying to translate one than by writing an essay about it.

SR: *How does translation relate to your own work now?*
PA: At this point hardly at all. In the beginning, it occupied a central place for me, but then, as time went on, it became more and more marginal. My first translations years ago of modern French poets were real acts of discovery, labors of love. Then I went through a long period when I earned my living by doing translations. That was a completely different matter. I had nothing to do with choosing the texts. The publishers would tell me that they needed a translation of such and such a book, and I would do it. It was very draining work and had nothing to do with literature or my own writing. History books, anthropology books, art books. You grind out so many pages a day, and it puts bread on the table. Eventually, I stopped doing it to save my sanity. For the past five or six years, I've tried

to limit myself to things that I am passionately interested in – works that I have discovered and want to share with other people. Joubert's notebooks, for example, or the Anatole fragments by Mallarmé. I find both those works extraordinary, unlike anything I have ever read. The same with the book about high-wire walking by Philippe Petit, which was published last summer. I did it because Philippe is a friend and because he is one of the most remarkable artists I know. If those books are not exactly connected to my writing, they still belong to my inner world. But the act of translating in itself is no longer the adventure for me that it once was. There are sublimely talented translators out there in America today – Manheim, Rabassa, Wilbur, Mandelbaum, to name just a few. But I don't think of myself as belonging to the fraternity of translators. I'm just someone who likes to follow his nose, and more often than not this leads me into some odd corners. Occasionally, I will stumble onto something that excites me enough to want to translate it, but these generally seem to be eccentric and peculiar works – works that correspond to my own eccentric and peculiar tastes!

1985

INTERVIEW WITH JOSEPH MALLIA

JOSEPH MALLIA: *In your book of essays* The Art of Hunger *you cite Samuel Beckett as saying, 'There will be a new form.' Is your work an example of that new form?*

PAUL AUSTER: It seems that everything comes out a little strangely in my books, that they don't quite resemble other books, but whether they're 'new' in any sense, I really can't say. It's not my ambition to think about it. So I suppose the answer is yes and no. At this point I'm not even thinking about anything beyond writing the books themselves. They impose themselves on me, so it's not my choice. The only thing that really matters, it seems to me, is saying the thing that has to be said. If it really has to be said, it will create its own form.

JM: *All of your early work, from the 1970s, is poetry. What brought about this switch in genres, what made you want to write prose?*

PA: Starting from a very early age, writing novels was always my ambition. When I was a student in college, in fact, I spent a great deal more time writing prose than poetry. But the projects and ideas that I took on were too large for me, too ambitious, and I could never get a grip on them. By concentrating on a smaller form I felt that I was able to make more progress. Years went by, and writing poetry became such an obsession that I stopped thinking about anything else. I wrote very short, compact lyrical poems that usually took me months to complete. They were very dense, especially in the beginning – coiled in on themselves like fists – but over the years they gradually began to open up, until I finally felt that they were heading in the direction of narrative. I don't think of myself as having made a break from poetry. All my work is of a piece, and the move into prose was the last step in a slow and natural evolution.

JM: *As a younger writer, who were the modern writers you were interested in?*

PA: Of prose writers, unquestionably Kafka and Beckett. They both had a tremendous hold over me. In the same sense, the influence of Beckett was so strong that I couldn't see my way beyond it. Among poets, I was very attracted to contemporary French poetry and the American Objectivists, particularly George Oppen, who became a close friend. And the German poet Paul Celan, who in my opinion is the finest post-War poet in any language. Of older writers, there were Hölderlin and Leopardi, the essays of Montaigne, and Cervantes' *Don Quixote*, which has remained a great source for me.

JM: *But in the '70s you also wrote a great number of articles and essays about other writers.*

PA: Yes, that's true. There was a period in the middle '70s in particular when I found myself eager to test my own ideas about writers in print. It's one thing to read and admire somebody's work, but it's quite another to marshal your thoughts about that writer into something coherent. The people I wrote about – Laura Riding, Edmond Jabès, Louis Wolfson, Knut Hamsun, and others – were writers I felt a need to respond to. I never considered myself a reviewer, but simply one writer trying to talk about others. Having to write for publication disciplined me, I think, and convinced me that ultimately I was able to write prose. So in some sense those little pieces of literary journalism were the training ground for the novels.

JM: *Your first prose book was* The Invention of Solitude, *which was an autobiographical book.*

PA: I don't think of it as an autobiography so much as a meditation about certain questions, using myself as the central character. The book is divided into two sections, which were written separately, with a gap of about a year between the two. The first, *Portrait of an Invisible Man*, was written in response to my father's death. He simply dropped dead one day, unexpectedly, after being in perfect health, and the shock of it left me with so many unanswered questions about him that I felt I had no choice but to sit down and try to put something on paper. In the act of trying to write about him, I began to realize how problematical it is to presume to know anything about anyone else. While that piece is filled with specific details, it still seems to me not so much an attempt at biography but an exploration of how one might begin to speak about another person, and whether or not it is even possible.

The second part grew out of the first and was a response to it. It gave me a great deal of trouble, especially in terms of organization. I began writing it in the first person, as the first part had been written, but couldn't make any headway with it. This part was even more personal than the first, but the more deeply I descended into the material, the more distanced I became from it. In order to write about myself, I had to treat myself as though I were someone else. It was only when I started all over again in the third person that I began to see my way out of the impasse. The astonishing thing, I think, is that at the moment when you are most truly alone, when you truly enter a state of solitude, that is the moment when you are not alone anymore, when you start to feel your connection with others. I believe I even quote Rimbaud in that book, 'Je est un autre' – I is another – and I take that sentence quite literally. In the process of writing or thinking about yourself, you actually become someone else.

JM: *Not only is the narrative voice of* The Book of Memory *different, but the structure is different as well.*

PA: The central question in the second part was memory. So in some sense everything that happens in it is simultaneous. But writing is sequential, it unfolds over time. So my greatest problem was in trying to put things in the correct order.

The point was to be as honest as possible in every sentence. I wanted to write a work that was completely exposed. I didn't want to hide anything. I wanted to break down for myself the boundary between living and writing as much as I could. That's not to say that a lot of literary effort didn't go into the book, but the impulses are all very immediate and pressing. With everything I do, it seems that I just get so inside it, I can't think about anything else. And writing the book becomes real for me. I was talking about myself in *The Book of Memory*, but by tracking specific instances of my own mental process, perhaps I was doing something that other people could understand as well.

JM: *Yes, that's how it worked for me.* The Book of Memory *dwells on coincidences, strange intersections of events in the world. This is also true in the novels of* The New York Trilogy.

PA: Yes, I believe the world is filled with strange events. Reality is a great deal more mysterious than we ever give it credit for. In that sense, the *Trilogy* grows directly out of *The Invention of Solitude*. On the most personal level, I think of *City of Glass* as an homage to my wife. It's a kind of fictitious subterranean autobiography, an attempt to imagine what my life would have been like if I hadn't met her. That's why I had to appear in the book as myself, but at the same time Auster is also Quinn, but in a different universe. . . .

The opening scene in the book is something that actually happened to me. I was living alone at the time, and one night the telephone rang and the person on the other end asked for the Pinkerton Detective Agency. I told him that he had the wrong number, of course, but the same person called back the next night with the same question. When I hung up the phone the second time, I asked myself what would have happened if I had said 'Yes'. That was the genesis of the book, and I went on from there.

JM: *Reviews of the book seem to emphasize the mystery elements of* The New York Trilogy, *making it out to be a gloss on the mystery genre. Did you feel that you were writing a mystery novel?*

PA: Not at all. Of course I used certain elements of detective fiction. Quinn, after all, writes detective novels and takes on the identity of someone he thinks is a detective. But I felt I was using those elements for such different ends, for things that had so little to do with detective stories, and I was somewhat disappointed by the emphasis that was put on them. That's not to say that I have anything against the genre. The mystery, after all, is one of the oldest and most compelling forms of storytelling, and any number of works can be placed in that category: *Oedipus Rex, Crime and Punishment*, a whole range of twentieth-century novels. In America, there's no question that people like Raymond Chandler and James M. Cain are legitimate writers, writers who have contributed something important to the language. It's a mistake to look down on the popular forms.

You have to be open to everything, to be willing to take inspiration from any and all sources. In the same way that Cervantes used chivalric romances as the starting point for *Don Quixote*, or the way that Beckett used the standard vaudeville routine as the framework for *Waiting for Godot*, I tried to use certain genre conventions to get to another place, another place altogether.

JM: *The problem of identity, right?*
PA: Exactly. The question of who is who and whether or not we are who we think we are. The whole process that Quinn undergoes in that book – and the characters in the other two, as well – is one of stripping away to some barer condition in which we have to face up to who we are. Or who we aren't. It finally comes to the same thing.

JM: *And the detective is somebody who's supposed to deal with the problems we have in maintaining a conventional identity. He deals with the messy edges of reality. Like, 'My wife, she's not doing what she's supposed to –'*
PA: Right, exactly – or 'Somebody's missing'. So the detective really is a very compelling figure, a figure we all understand. He's the seeker after truth, the problem-solver, the one who tries to figure things out. But what if, in the course of trying to figure it out, you just unveil more mysteries? I suppose maybe that's what happens in the books.

The books have to do with the idea of mystery in several ways. We're surrounded by things we don't understand, by mysteries, and in the books there are people who suddenly come face to face with them. It becomes more apparent that they're surrounded by things they don't know or understand. So in that sense there might be some psychological resonance. Even though the situations aren't strictly realistic, they might follow some realistic psychology. These are things that we all feel – that confusion, that lack of knowing what it is that surrounds us.

JM: *I saw the protagonists dropping into a kind of necessity, suddenly, and putting personal life aside, driven by some extraordinary hunger. It has almost religious undertones to it. I remember reading a review by Fanny Howe in the* Boston Globe, *and she said that the book is about a kind of gnosis – 'grace among the fallen'.*

PA: 'Religious' might not be the word I would use, but I agree that these books are mostly concerned with spiritual questions, the search for spiritual grace. At some point or another, all three characters undergo a form of humiliation, of degradation, and perhaps that is a necessary stage in discovering who we are.

Each novel in the *Trilogy*, I suppose, is about a kind of passionate excess. Quinn's story in *City of Glass* alludes to *Don Quixote*, and the questions raised in the two books are very similar: what is the line between madness and creativity, what is the line between the real and the imaginary, is Quinn crazy to do what he does or not? For a time, I toyed with the idea of using an epigraph at the beginning of *City of Glass*. It comes from Wittgenstein: 'And it also means something to talk of "living in the pages of a book".'

In *Ghosts*, the spirit of Thoreau is dominant – another kind of passionate excess. The idea of living a solitary life, of living with a kind of monastic intensity – and all the dangers that entails. Walden Pond in the heart of the city. In his *American Notebook*, Hawthorne wrote an extraordinary and luminous sentence about Thoreau that has never left me. 'I think he means to live like an Indian among us.' That sums up the project better than anything else I've read. The determination to reject everyday American life, to go against the grain, to discover a more solid foundation for oneself. . . . In *The Locked Room*, by the way, the name Fanshawe is a direct reference to Hawthorne. *Fanshawe* was the title of Hawthorne's first novel. He wrote it when he was very young, and not long after it was published, he turned against it in revulsion and tried to destroy every copy he could get his hands on. Fortunately, a few of them survived . . .

JM: *In* Ghosts, Blue, *in effect, loses his whole life in taking the case, and the narrator in* The Locked Room *goes through that terrible experience in Paris –*

PA: But in the end, he manages to resolve the question for himself – more or less. He finally comes to accept his own life, to understand that no matter how bewitched or haunted he is, he has to accept reality as it is, to tolerate the presence of ambiguities within himself. That's what happens to him with relation to Fanshawe. He hasn't slain the dragon, he's let the dragon move into the house with him. That's why he destroys the notebook in the last scene.

JM: *And the reader feels it. We're inside him.*

PA: The one thing I try to do in all my books is to leave enough room in the prose for the reader to inhabit it. Because I finally believe it's the reader who writes the book and not the writer. In my own case as a reader (and I've certainly read more books than I've written!), I find that I almost invariably appropriate scenes and situations from a book and graft them onto my own experiences – or vice versa. In reading a book like *Pride and Prejudice*, for example, I realized at a certain point that all events were set in the house I grew up in as a child. No matter how specific a writer's description of a place might be, I always seem to twist it into something I'm familiar with. I've asked a number of my friends if this happens to them when they read fiction as well. For some yes, for others no. I think this probably has a lot to do with one's relation to language, how one responds to words printed on a page. Whether the words are just symbols, or whether they are passage-ways into our unconscious.

There's a way in which a writer can do too much, over-whelming the reader with so many details that he no longer has any air to breathe. Think of a typical passage in a novel. A character walks into a room. As a writer, how much of that room do you want to talk about? The possibilities are infinite. You can give the color of the curtains, the wall-paper pattern, the objects on the coffee table, the reflection of the light in the mirror. But how much of this is really necessary? Is the novelist's job simply to reproduce physi-cal sensations for their own sake? When I write, the story is always uppermost in my mind, and I feel that everything must be sacrificed to it. All the elegant passages, all the curious details, all the so-called beautiful writing – if they are not truly relevant to what I am trying to say, then they have to go. It's all in the voice. You're telling a story, after all, and your job is to make people want to go on listening to your tale. The slightest distraction or wander-ing leads to boredom, and if there's one thing we all hate in books, it's losing interest, feeling bored, not caring about the next sentence. In the end, you don't only write the books you need to write, but you write the books you would like to read yourself.

JM: *Is there a method to it?*

PA: No. The deeper I get into my own work, the less engag-ing theoretical problems have become. When you look back on the works that have moved you, you find that they have always been written out of some kind of necessity. There's something calling out to you, some human call, that makes you want to listen to the work. In the end, it probably has very little to do with literature.

Georges Bataille wrote about this in his preface to *Le Bleu du Ciel*. I refer to it in *The Art of Hunger*, in an essay on the schizophrenic Wolfson. He said that every real book comes from a moment of rage, and then he asked: 'How can we read works that we don't feel compelled to read?' I believe he's absolutely correct: there's always some indefinable something that makes you attend to a writer's work – you can never put your finger on it, but that something is what makes all the difference.

JM: *In other words the writer has to be haunted by his story before he can write it.*

PA: In my own experience I've often lived for years with the ideas for books before I could manage to write them. *In The Country of Last Things* is a novel I started writing back in the days when I was a college student. The idea of an unknowable place ... it got under my skin and I couldn't let go of it. I would pick up the manuscript, work on it for a while, and then put it down. The essential thing was to capture her voice, and when I couldn't hear it anymore, I would have to stop. I must have started the book thirty times. Each time it was somewhat different than the time before, but the essential situation was always the same.

JM: *In the same way that some reviewers classified* The New York Trilogy *as a mystery, there were many articles about this book that classified it as apocalyptic science fiction.*

PA: That was the farthest thing from my mind while I was writing it. In fact, my private, working subtitle for the book was 'Anna Blume Walks Through the 20th Century'. I feel that it's very much a book about our own moment, our own era, and many of the incidents are things that have actually happened. For example, the pivotal scene in which Anna is lured into a human slaughterhouse is based on something I read about the siege of Leningrad during World War II. These things actually happened. And in many cases, reality is far more terrible than anything we can imagine. Even the garbage system that I describe at such length was inspired by an article I once read about the present-day garbage system in Cairo. Admittedly, the book takes on these things from a somewhat oblique angle, and the country Anna goes to might not be immediately recognizable, but I feel that this is where we live. It could be that we've become so accustomed to it that we no longer see it.

JM: *What are you working on now?*
PA: I'm coming close to the end of a novel called *Moon Palace*. It's the longest book I've ever written and probably the one most rooted in a specific time and place. The action begins in 1969 and doesn't get much beyond 1971. At bottom, I suppose, it's a story about families and generation, a kind of *David Copperfield* novel, and it's something that I've been wanting to write for a long time. As with the last book, it's gone through many changes. The pages pile up, but God knows what it will look like when it's finished. . . . Whenever I complete a book, I'm filled with a feeling of immense disgust and disappointment. It's almost a physical collapse. I'm so disappointed by my feeble efforts that I can't believe I've actually spent so much time and accomplished so little. It takes years before I'm able to accept what I've done – to realize that this was the best I could do. But I never like to look at the things I've written. The past is the past, and there's nothing I can do about it any more. The only thing that counts is the project I'm working on now.

JM: *Beckett once said in one of his stories, 'No sooner is the ink dry than it revolts me.'*

PA: You can't say it any better than that.

1987

LARRY McCAFFERY: *At one point in* Moon Palace, *Marco Fogg says that art's purpose is 'penetrating the world and finding one's place in it'. Is that what writing does for you?*

PAUL AUSTER: Sometimes. I often wonder why I write. It's not simply to create beautiful objects or entertaining stories. It's an activity I seem to need in order to stay alive. I feel terrible when I'm not doing it. It's not that writing brings me a lot of pleasure – but *not* doing it is worse.

SINDA GREGORY: *Your books have always relied more on chance and synchronicity to move their plots forward than the sorts of causality found in most fiction: this is even more apparent in your two new novels,* Moon Palace *and* The Music of Chance. *Is this foregrounding of chance a result of your own sense of how life operates (your 'personal philosophy')? Or does it have more to do with your sense that this approach has interesting aesthetic applications?*

PA: From an aesthetic point of view, the introduction of chance elements in fiction probably creates as many problems as it solves. I've come in for a lot of abuse from critics because of it. In the strictest sense of the word, I consider myself a realist. Chance is a part of reality: we are continually shaped by the forces of coincidence, the unexpected occurs with almost numbing regularity in all our lives. And yet there's a widely held notion that novels shouldn't stretch the imagination too far. Anything that appears 'implausible' is necessarily taken to be forced, artificial, 'unrealistic'. I don't know what reality these people have been living in, but it certainly isn't my reality. In some perverse way, I believe they've spent too much time reading books. They're so immersed in the conventions of so-called realistic fiction that their sense of reality has been distorted. Everything's been smoothed out in these novels, robbed of its singularity, boxed into a predictable world of cause and effect. Anyone with the wit to get his nose out of his book and study what's actually in front of him will understand that this realism is a complete sham. To put it another way: truth is stranger than fiction. What I am after, I suppose, is to write fiction as strange as the world I live in.

LM: *I'd say your books don't use coincidence in an effort to 'smooth things over' or to create the usual realist's manipulated illusion that everything can be explained. Your books seem more fundamentally 'about' mystery and coincidence, so that these operate almost as governing principles that are constantly clashing with causality and rationality.*

PA: Precisely. When I talk about coincidence, I'm not referring to a desire to manipulate. There's a good deal of that in bad eighteenth- and nineteenth-century fiction: mechanical plot devices, the urge to tie everything up, the happy endings in which everyone turns out to be related to everyone else. No, what I'm talking about is the presence of the unpredictable, the utterly bewildering nature of human experience. From one moment to the next, anything can happen. Our life-long certainties about the world can be demolished in a single second. In philosophical terms, I'm talking about the powers of contingency. Our lives don't really belong to us, you see – they belong to the world, and in spite of our efforts to make sense of it, the world is a place beyond our understanding. We brush up against these mysteries all the time. The result can be truly terrifying – but it can also be comical.

SG: *What sorts of things are you thinking of – a small thing, like someone getting a phone call to the wrong number (which sets the plot of* City of Glass *in motion)? Or something more outlandish, like meeting your long-lost father by accident in* Moon Palace?

PA: I'm thinking of both small things and large things. Meeting three people named George on the same day. Or checking into a hotel and being given a room with the same number as your address at home. Seven or eight years ago, my wife and I were invited to a dinner party in New York, and there was an exceedingly charming man at the table – very urbane, full of intelligence and humor, a dazzling talker who had all the guests captivated with his stories. My wife had grown up in a small town in Minnesota, and at one point she actually said to herself: this is why I moved to New York, to meet people like this. Later on in the evening, we all started talking about our childhoods and where we had grown up. As it turned out, the man who had so enthralled her, the man who had struck her as the very embodiment of New York sophistication, came from the same little town in Minnesota that she did. The same town! It was astonishing – like something straight out of an O. Henry story.

These are coincidences, and it's impossible to know what to make of them. You think of a long-lost friend, someone you haven't seen in ten years, and two hours later you run into him on the street. Things like that happen to me all the time. Just two or three years ago, a woman who had been reading my books wrote to me to say that she was going to be in New York and would like to meet me. We had been corresponding for some time, and I welcomed the chance to talk to her in person. Unfortunately, there was a conflict. I already had an appointment with someone else for that day, and I couldn't make it. I was supposed to meet my friend at three or four o'clock in a delicatessen in midtown Manhattan. So I went to the restaurant – which was rather empty at that hour, since it was neither lunchtime nor dinnertime – and not fifteen minutes after we sat down, a woman with an absolutely startled expression on her face walked up to me and asked if I was Paul Auster. It turned out to be the same woman from Iowa who had written me those letters, the same woman I hadn't been able to meet with because I was going to this restaurant. And so I wound up meeting her anyway – in the very place where I hadn't been able to meet her!

Chance? Destiny? Or simple mathematics, an example of probability theory at work? It doesn't matter what you call it. Life is full of such events. And yet there are critics who would fault a writer for using that episode in a novel. Too bad for them. As a writer of novels, I feel morally obligated to incorporate such events into my books, to write about the world as I experience it – not as someone else tells me it's supposed to be. The unknown is rushing in on top of us at every moment. As I see it, my job is to keep myself open to these collisions, to watch out for all these mysterious goings-on in the world.

LM: *When you say that your job as a writer is to open yourself to these collisions that are really occurring around you, does this imply that your works are usually inspired in some fairly direct way from the mysteries you've actually experienced – or is the autobiographical basis of your work less literal?*

PA: Essentially, I'm a very intuitive writer, which makes it difficult for me to talk about my work in any coherent way. There's no question that my books are full of references to my own life, but more often than not, I don't become aware of these references until after the fact. *Moon Palace* is a good case in point. It sounds more like an autobiography than any of my other novels, but the truth is that it's probably the least autobiographical novel I've ever written. Still, there are a number of private allusions buried in the story, but it was only after the book was finished that I began to see them.

The business about the boxes of books in the beginning, for example. Fogg receives these boxes from his Uncle Victor, and after his uncle dies, Fogg sells off the books to keep himself afloat. Well, it turns out that the image of those boxes must have been planted in my head way back in my early childhood. My mother's sister is married to Allen Mandelbaum, who is widely known now as the translator of Virgil and Dante. When I was five or six, my aunt and uncle went off to live in Italy and wound up staying there for twelve years. My uncle had an enormous library, and since we lived in a large house, he left his books with us for all the years he was gone. At first, they were stored in boxes in the attic, but after a while (I must have been nine or ten at that point), my mother began to worry that the books might get damaged up there. So one fine day she and I carried the boxes downstairs, opened them up, and put the books on shelves in the living room. Until then, our household had been largely devoid of books. Neither of my parents had gone to college, and neither of them was particularly interested in reading. Now, quite suddenly, literally overnight, I had a magnificent library at my disposal: all the classics, all the great poets, all the major novels. It opened up a whole new world to me. When I think back on it now, I realize that these boxes of books probably changed my life. Without them, I doubt I ever would have dreamed of becoming a writer.

The Edison material has deep roots in my past as well. Our house wasn't far from the Seton Hall University campus, and every two weeks I would go for a haircut at Rocco's Barbershop, which did a brisk business with the college students and the boys from the town. This was the late fifties, and everyone walked around in crewcuts then, which meant that you wound up going to the barbershop quite often. Anyway, it so happened that Rocco had been Thomas Edison's barber for many years, and hanging on a wall of the shop was a large framed portrait of Edison, along with a handwritten message from the great man himself. 'To my good friend Rocco,' it said. 'Genius is 1% inspiration, 99% perspiration. Thomas A. Edison.' I found it tremendously exciting that my barber was the same man who had once cut the hair of the inventor of the lightbulb. It was ennobling, somehow – to imagine that the hands touching my head had once touched the head of America's greatest genius. I used to think that ideas from Edison's brain had been transferred to Rocco's fingers – which meant that those ideas were now going into my brain! Edison became the hero of childhood, and each time I went for a haircut, I'd stare at his portrait and feel as though I were worshipping at a shrine.

Some years later, this beautiful myth of my boyhood shattered to pieces. It turned out that my father had once worked as an assistant in Edison's lab at Menlo park. He had been hired straight out of high school in 1929, but just a few weeks after he started the job, Edison discovered that he was Jewish and fired him. My idol turned out to be a vicious anti-Semite, a scoundrel who had done my father a terrible injustice. None of this is mentioned in *Moon Palace*, of course, but the unflattering references to Edison no doubt come from the personal animosity I developed for him. I won't bore you by citing other examples, but in some way the whole book is impregnated with subliminal connections of this sort. There's nothing unusual about that. All writers draw on their own lives to write their books; to a greater or lesser degree, every novel is autobiographical. What *is* interesting, however, is how the work of the imagination intersects with reality.

SG: *Do you mean that eerie sense that Borges kept writing about – the author who begins to find evidence of his writing somehow finding its way into the world? A big responsibility . . .*

PA: It can become quite disturbing at times, utterly uncanny. The very day I finished writing *The Music of Chance* – which is a book about walls and slavery and freedom – the Berlin Wall came down. There's no conclusion to be drawn from this, but every time I think of it, I start to shake.

Back in 1984, when I was in the middle of writing *The Locked Room*, I had to go to Boston for a few days. I already knew that the final scene in the book was going to take place in a house in Boston, at 9 Columbus Square, which happens to be a real address. The house is owned by good friends of mine, and I have slept there on many occasions over the past fifteen years or so. That's where I was going to stay this time as well, and I remember thinking how odd it would be to visit this house again now that I had fictionalized it for myself, had appropriated it into the realm of the imagination. I took the train to Boston, and when I arrived at South Station, I climbed into a cab and asked the driver to take me to 9 Columbus Square. The moment I gave him the address, he started to laugh. It turned out that he had once lived there himself – back in the 1940s, at a time when the building had been used as a boarding house. Not only that, but he had lived in the very room where my friend now had his study. For the rest of the ride, he told me stories about the people who had lived there, the woman who had owned it, and all the mischief that had gone on in the rooms I knew so well. Prostitution, pornographic films, drugs, crimes of every sort. It was all so odd, so mysterious. Even today, it's hard for me not to feel that I invented this cab driver myself, that he didn't materialize out of the pages of my own book. It was as if I had met the spirit of the place I was writing about. The ghost of 9 Columbus Square!

LM: *You told me once that in a certain way you felt all of your books were really 'the same book'. What book is that?*
PA: The story of my obsessions, I suppose. The saga of the things that haunt me. Like it or not, all my books seem to revolve around the same set of questions, the same human dilemmas. Writing is no longer an act of free will for me, it's a matter of survival. An image surges up inside me, and after a time I begin to feel cornered by it, to feel that I have no choice but to embrace it. A book starts to take shape after a series of such encounters.

SG: *Have you tried to figure out the specific source of these encounters?*
PA: Frankly, I'm never really certain where any of it comes from. I'm sure there are deep psychological explanations for most of it, but I'm not terribly interested in trying to track down the source of my ideas. Writing, in some sense, is an activity that helps me to relieve some of the pressure caused by these buried secrets. Hidden memories, traumas, childhood scars – there's no question that novels emerge from those inaccessible parts of ourselves.

Every once in a while, however, I'll have a glimmer or a sudden intuition about where something came from. But, as I said before, it always happens after the fact, after the book is finished, at a moment when the book no longer belongs to me. Just recently, as I was going through the manuscript of *The Music of Chance* for typographical errors, I had a revelation about one of the scenes that takes place toward the end of the novel: the moment when Nashe opens the door of the trailer and discovers Pozzi lying on the ground. As I read that passage – which goes on to describe how Nashe bends over the body and examines Pozzi to see if he is alive or dead – I understood that I was writing about something that had happened to me many years before. It was one of the most terrible moments in my life, an episode that has stayed with me ever since, and yet I wasn't aware of it at the time I composed that scene.

I was thirteen or fourteen years old and had been sent to a summer camp in upstate New York. One day, a group of about twenty of us went for a hike in the woods, accompanied by one or two counselors. We trekked for several miles, I remember, all of us in good spirits, when it suddenly began to rain. A moment later, the sky opened up, and we found ourselves in the middle of a ferocious downpour, a summer lightning storm punctuated by tremendous claps of thunder. It wasn't just some passing cloud. It was an out-and-out tempest, a monumental attack from the heavens. Lightning bolts were shooting down all around us, and there we were, stuck in the woods, with no shelter in sight. It became very terrifying, as though we had suddenly been caught in an aerial bombardment. One of the boys said that we would be safer if we got away from the trees, and so we began to scramble back toward a clearing we had passed a little while before. He was right, of course. In a lightning storm, you have to protect yourself by going to open ground. The problem in this case was that in order to enter the clearing, we had to crawl under a barbed wire fence. So, one by one, we crawled under the fence and made our way to what we thought would be safety. I was somewhere in the middle of the line, behind a boy named Ralph. Just as he was crawling under the fence, an enormous bolt of lightning struck the wire. I couldn't have been more than two feet away from him. He stopped, apparently stunned by the lightning, and I remember that I crawled under the fence at that point, inching under the wire to Ralph's left. Once I got through, I turned around and dragged him into the meadow to make room for the other boys. It didn't occur to me that he was seriously hurt. I figured that he had received a shock and would soon recover from it. Once we were all in the clearing, the lightning attack continued; the bolts were dancing around us like spears. Several of the boys were hit, and they lay there weeping and moaning on the ground. It was an awful scene, truly awful. Another boy and I stayed with Ralph the whole time, rubbing his hands to keep him warm, holding his tongue to make sure he didn't swallow it. His lips were turning blue, his skin was turning cold, but still, I kept thinking he would start coming around at any moment. He was dead, of course. He had been killed the instant the lightning had hit the fence – electrocuted, with an eight-inch burn across his back. But I didn't learn that until afterward, until after the storm had stopped.

LM: *That's the kind of experience you never leave behind completely.*

PA: No, never. I can't tell you how deeply it affected me. Not just the tragedy of a young boy losing his life like that – but the absolute suddenness of it, the fact that I could easily have been the one crawling under the fence when the lightning struck. Speaking about it now, I understand how crucial it was to me. In some sense, my entire attitude toward life was formed in those woods in upstate New York.

SG: *In retrospect, is that why* Moon Palace *winds up having those two critical scenes involving lightning?*

PA: There's no question that those storms refer to the storm I lived through, I'm certain of it. And there are other traces of that event in *Moon Palace*. The passage when Effing watches over Byrne's body in the Utah desert. Clearly I was reliving the experience of watching over the dead boy's body in the woods . . .

What I am trying to say, I suppose, is that the material that haunts me, the material that I feel compelled to write about, is dredged up from the depths of my own memories. But even after that material is given to me, I can't always be sure where it comes from.

LM: *How do you balance this sense of feeling* compelled *to write about these things, your desire to leave yourself open, creatively, to these powerful resonances, versus your goal as an artist to control them, to shape them into an aesthetic arrangement?*

PA: I don't mean to imply that my books are nothing but an outpouring of my unconscious. There's art involved as well, and effort, and a very precise sense of the kinds of feelings I am trying to convey. To say that 'all my books are the same book' is probably too simple. What I mean is that all my books are connected by their common source, by the preoccupations they share. But each book belongs to its central character: Quinn, Blue, the narrator of *The Locked Room*, Anna Blume, Fogg, Nashe. Each one of these people thinks differently, speaks differently, writes differently from all the others. But each one is also a part of myself – which probably goes without saying. If all these books were put together in one volume, they would form the book of my life so far, a multi-faceted picture of who I am. But there's still more to come, I hope. If you think of the imagination as a continent, then each book would be

an individual country. The map is still quite sketchy at this
point, with many gaps and unexplored territories. But if
I'm able to keep going long enough, perhaps all the blanks
will eventually be filled in.

sg: *On the other hand, you frequently seem to return to the same
'terrain', even if it's located on different literary continents. For
example, there's a recurrent motif in several of your books (I'm
thinking of* City of Glass, Moon Palace *and* The Music of
Chance) *of the windfall or inheritance that creates a suspension
of the daily routine for the main character, followed by a gradual
dissipation of the money until the character is left with nothing.
This sounds almost like a starving artist's fantasy, but since the
process is described so vividly and convincingly, I wonder if it
might have a basis in your autobiography . . .*

pa: As a matter of fact, I did receive an inheritance after
my father died eleven years ago. It wasn't a tremendous
amount of money as far as inheritances go, but it made a
huge difference, it was enough to change my life entirely.
I was pushing thirty-two at the time, and in the ten years
since graduating from college I had been scraping along as
best I could, often in very miserable circumstances. There
were long stretches of time when I had nothing, when I
was literally on the brink of catastrophe. The year before
my father died was a particularly bad period. I had a small
child, a crumbling marriage, and a miniscule income that
amounted to no more than a fraction of what we needed.
I became desperate, and for more than a year I wrote almost
nothing. I couldn't think about anything but money. Half-
crazed by the pressure of it all, I began devising various
get-rich-quick schemes. I invented a game (a card baseball
game – which was actually quite good) and spent close to
six months trying to sell it. When that failed, I sat down
and wrote a pseudonymous detective novel in record time,

about three months. It was eventually published, but it only brought in about two thousand dollars, which was hardly the kind of money I had been hoping for.

At another point, I made some inquiries about getting a job as a sports writer, but nothing came of that either. As a last resort, I even broke down and applied for a job as a teacher. A full load of freshman composition courses at Dutchess Community College for $8000 a year. This was the worst thing I could imagine, but I swallowed my pride and took the plunge. I thought my credentials were decent. I had an M.A. from Columbia, I had published two or three books of poetry, I had translated quite a bit, had written articles for *The New York Review of Books*, *Harper's*, and so on. But it turned out that there were three hundred applicants for that miserable job, and without any prior experience, I didn't have a chance. I was rejected on the spot. I don't think I've ever been closer to feeling that I was at the end of my rope. Then, out of nowhere, with absolutely no warning at all, my father dropped dead of a heart attack and I inherited some money. That money changed everything for me; it set my life on an entirely different course.

LM: *Your early published creative works were nearly all poems. Wasn't it just after the death of your father that you first started writing prose – the materials that eventually became* The Invention of Solitude?

PA: Not exactly. Although you might say that it was only then that I began to think of myself as a prose writer. But the fact is that I had always dreamed of writing novels. My first published works were poems, and for ten years or so I published only poems, but all along I spent nearly as much time writing prose. I wrote hundreds and hundreds of pages, I filled up dozens of notebooks. It's just that I wasn't satisfied with it, and I never showed it to anyone. But the ideas for several of the novels I eventually published – at least in some kind of preliminary form – came to me back then, as far back as 1969 and 1970. I'm thinking particularly of *In The Country of Last Things* and *Moon Palace*, but also certain parts of *City of Glass*. The crazy speech about *Don Quixote*, the maps of Stillman's footsteps, the crackpot theories about America and the Tower of Babel – all that was cooked up when I was still in my early twenties.

SG: *But at some point you fairly consciously decided to shift your focus away from prose to poetry. What was behind this decision?*
PA: It was like someone trying to will himself to break a bad habit. By about the mid '70s, I stopped writing fiction altogether. I felt that I was wasting my time, that I would never get anywhere with it, and so I decided to restrict myself exclusively to poetry.

LM: *Was it really so exclusive, though? Wasn't this about the time your first critical essays began appearing?*
PA: Yes, I suppose I failed to break the habit. I continued writing prose anyway, quite a bit of it, in fact. Critical prose, articles, book reviews. Between 1974 and 1979, I must have written twenty-five or thirty pieces. It started right after I returned to New York. I had just spent four years living in France, and right before I left, an American friend of mine in Paris who knew Bob Silvers of *The New York Review of Books* suggested that I contact him once I returned. I eventually did, and when I proposed writing an article about Louis Wolfson's book *Le Schizo et les Langues*, he said go ahead. He made no promises, of course, but I remember that he offered to pay me something even if they didn't publish it, which I found very generous and uncalled-for. It turned out that he liked the article, and I wound up writing a number of others for him. They were

mostly on poets – Laura Riding, Jabès, Ungaretti, and so on. Bob Silvers was an excellent editor – tough, respectful, very businesslike and very enthusiastic – and I'm still grateful to him for having given me a chance.

LM: *Did you find any of the same kinds of pleasures writing those critical articles that you received from your creative work?*
PA: I never thought of myself as a critic or literary journalist, even when I was doing a lot of critical pieces. Eventually, I started writing articles for other magazines as well. *Harper's, Saturday Review, Parnassus, The San Francisco Review of Books*, I can't remember all of them. I never accepted assignments or did pieces to order. I only wrote about writers who interested me, and in nearly every case I was the one who suggested the article to the editor – not the other way around. I looked on those pieces as an opportunity to articulate some of my ideas about writing and literature, to map out some kind of aesthetic position. In effect, I could have accomplished the same thing by keeping a journal, but I felt it was more interesting and challenging to throw my thoughts out into a public arena. I wasn't able to cheat. Everything had to be stated with absolute clarity: there was no room for vague impressions. All in all, I feel it was a useful apprenticeship. I wasn't writing fiction, but I was writing prose, and the experience of working on those articles proved to me that I was gradually learning how to express myself.

SG: *How was your poetry evolving during this period?*
PA: It was beginning to change, beginning to open up. I had started out by writing poems that resembled clenched fists; they were short and dense and obscure, as compact and hermetic as Delphic oracles. But by the mid-'70s I could feel them taking on a new direction. The breath became somewhat longer, the propositions became some-

what more discursive. At times, a certain prose tonality began to creep in. In 1976 and 1977, I wrote four one-act plays, wondering if this wouldn't be the proper medium for these new urges that were growing inside me. One of them, to my everlasting regret, was even performed. There's no point in talking about that now – except to say that the memory of that performance still pains me. But another of those plays eventually came to life again. Six years later, I went back to it and reworked it into a piece of prose fiction. That was where *Ghosts* came from, the second novel of *The New York Trilogy*.

LM: *Was there any particular breakthrough moment for you in terms of your prose – something that made you realize you could work in this form? Or was it more a matter of one thing leading to another – the essay, the plays, and so on – until you felt comfortable with it?*

PA: It was both, I think, if such a thing is possible. But first came all the emotional and financial hardships I mentioned before. I barely wrote anything for close to a year. My wife and I were grinding out translations to put food on the table, and the rest of the time I was pursuing my half-baked money schemes. There were moments when I thought I was finished, when I thought I would never write another word. Then, in December of 1978, I happened to go to an open rehearsal of a dance piece choreographed by the friend of a friend, and something happened to me. A revelation, an epiphany – I don't know what to call it. Something happened, and a whole world of possibilities suddenly opened up to me. I think it was the absolute fluidity of what I was seeing, the continual motion of the dancers as they moved around the floor. It filled me with immense happiness. The simple fact of watching men and women moving through space filled me with something close to euphoria. The very next day, I sat down and started writing *White Spaces*, a little work of no identifiable genre – which was an attempt on my part to translate the experience of that dance performance into words. It was a liberation for me, a tremendous letting go, and I look back on it now as the bridge between writing poetry and writing prose. That was the piece that convinced me I still had it in me to be a writer. But everything was going to be different now. A whole new period of my life was about to begin.

It's very strange, but I remember finishing that piece on January fourteenth. I went to sleep very late that night, around two or three in the morning. At eight o'clock the phone rang, and there was one of my uncles on the other end of the line, telling me that my father had died during the night. . . .

LM: *And along with that news came the inheritance.*

PA: Yes, then came the inheritance. The money gave me a cushion, and for the first time in my life I had the time to write, to take on long projects without worrying about how I was going to pay the rent. In some sense, all the novels I've written have come out of that money my father left me. It gave me two or three years, and that was enough to get me on my feet again. It's impossible to sit down and write without thinking about it. It's a terrible equation, finally. To think that my father's death saved my life.

SG: *The way you describe this movement – from initially writing prose, to abandoning it in favor of poetry when you felt you had failed at prose, to returning to it almost triumphantly during this moment of conversion – it almost sounds as if all along you had strong personal and aesthetic preferences for prose forms. If that's the case, how do you feel about the poetry you wrote during that period?*

PA: What it boils down to, I think, is a question of scope. It was a gradual process, but at the same time there was also a leap, a last little jump right at the end.

I remain very attached to the poetry I wrote, I still stand by it. In the final analysis, it could even be the best work I've ever done. But there's a fundamental difference between the two activities, at least in the way I've approached them. In some sense, poetry is like taking still photographs, whereas prose is like filming with a movie camera. Film is the medium for both those arts – but the results are totally different. In the same way, words are the medium for both poetry and prose, but they create entirely different experiences, both for the writer and the reader.

SG: *In other words, prose is able to encompass a lot more for you.*
PA: That's essentially it. My poems were a quest for what I would call a uni-vocal expression. They expressed what I felt at any given moment, as if I'd never felt anything before and would never feel anything again. They were concerned with essences, with bedrock beliefs, and their aim was always to achieve a purity and consistency of language. Prose, on the other hand, gives me a chance to articulate my conflicts and contradictions. Like everyone else, I am a multiple being, and I embody a whole range of attitudes and responses to the world. Depending on my mood, the same event can make me laugh or make me cry; it can inspire anger or compassion or indifference. Writing prose allows me to include all of these responses. I no longer have to choose among them.

LM: *That sounds like Bakhtin's notion of 'the dialogic imagination', with the novel arising out of this welter of conflicting but dynamic voices and opinions. Heteroglossia . . .*
PA: Exactly. Of all the theories of the novel, Bakhtin's strikes

me as the most brilliant, the one that comes closest to understanding the complexity and the magic of the form.

It probably also explains why it's so rare for a young person to write a good novel. You have to grow into yourself before you can take on the demands of fiction. I've been talking about it in theoretical and literary terms, but there's also the simple fact of growing older, of acquiring a better sense of who you are.

SG: *I know you had started other books before* City of Glass, *but one thing that struck me in reading that book was how* fully *formed this literary sensibility seemed to be for somebody just publishing his first novel. Were there some private, personal factors at work, beyond the death of your father, that helped you mature as a writer and as an individual, so that you were in fact ready to write that first novel?*

PA: I'm certain that having children has had a lot to do with it. Becoming a parent connects you to a world beyond yourself, to the continuum of generations, to the inevitability of your own death. You understand that you exist in time, and after that you can no longer look at yourself in the same way. It's impossible to take yourself as seriously as you once did. You begin to let go, and in that letting go – at least in my case – you can find yourself wanting to tell stories.

When my son was born twelve years ago, Charlie Simic, who's been a close friend for a long time, wrote me a letter of congratulations in which he said, 'Children are wonderful. If I didn't have kids, I'd walk around thinking I was Rimbaud all the time.' He put his finger right on the heart of the experience.

This past summer, something funny happened to me that threw this whole question of children and writing into very sharp focus. We rented a house in Vermont for two months, an old fallen-down place in the middle of nowhere, a wonderful refuge. I was still writing *The Music of Chance* then, and every morning I'd walk over to a little outbuilding on the property to work on the book. It was about twenty or thirty yards from the house, and the kids and their friends would often play in the area between the buildings. Right at the end of the summer, I was coming to the end of the first draft. As it happened, I finished on the day before we were supposed to head back to New York. I wrote the last sentence at about twelve or twelve-thirty in the afternoon, and I remember standing up from the table and saying to myself: 'You've finally done it, old man. For once in your life, you've written something halfway decent.' I felt good, really very good – which is something that almost never happens to me when I think about my work. I lit a cigar and opened the door to step out into the sun, wanting to savor the triumph for a few minutes before I returned to the house. So there I was, standing on the steps of my little shack, telling myself what a genius I was, when all of a sudden I looked up and saw my two-year old daughter in front of the house. She was stark naked (she scarcely wore any clothes all summer) and at that moment she was squatting over some stones and taking a shit. She saw me looking at her and began shouting very happily: 'Look at me, daddy! Look at what I'm doing!' So, rather than being able to bask in my own brilliance, I had to clean up my daughter's mess. That was the first thing I did after finishing my book (*Laughs*). Thirty seconds of glory, and then right back to earth. I can't be sure if Sophie was offering me a not-so-subtle form of literary criticism, or if she was simply making a philosophical statement about the equality of all creative acts. One way or the other, she knocked me off my cloud, and I was very grateful to her for it.

LM: *You mentioned earlier that all of your books are finally about yourself, that they are all exploring parts of your inner terrain.* City of Glass *supplies a lot of hints that it is in fact very much a book about you: not only do 'you' literally appear by name in the book, but everyone Quinn meets – all these doubles and mirrors of his lost wife and family – seems to reflect back to us Quinn's psychic dilemmas. And presumably yours. Had the experience of writing about yourself so prismatically in* The Invention of Solitude *helped prepare you, in a sense, for writing about yourself in the way you did in your novel?*

PA: I think so. Yes, most definitely. In some sense, *City of Glass* was a direct response to *The Invention of Solitude*, particularly the second part, the section called 'The Book of Memory'. But, in spite of the evidence, I wouldn't actually say that I was 'writing about myself' in either book. *The Invention of Solitude* is autobiographical, of course, but I don't feel that I was telling the story of my life so much as using myself to explore certain questions that are common to us all: how we think, how we remember, how we carry our pasts around with us at every moment. I was looking at myself in the same way a scientist studies a laboratory animal. I was no more than a little gray rat, a guinea pig stuck in the cage of my own consciousness. The book wasn't written as a form of therapy; it was an attempt to turn myself inside-out and examine what I was made of. Myself, yes – but myself as anyone, myself as everyone. Even the first part, which is ostensibly about my father, is finally concerned with something larger than one man's life. It's about the question of biography, about whether it's in fact possible for one person to talk to another person. *The Locked Room* picks up this problem again and approaches it from a somewhat different angle.

SG: *Given what you've just said, I would have assumed you*

would have tried to prevent your audience from reading City of Glass *as a disguised autobiography. Instead you introduce this possibility, and play with it in various ways. Why?*

PA: I think it stemmed from a desire to implicate myself in the machinery of the book. I don't mean my autobiographical self, I mean my author self, that mysterious other who lives inside me and puts my name on the covers of books. What I was hoping to do, in effect, was to take my name off the cover and put it inside the story. I wanted to open up the process, to break down walls, to expose the plumbing. There's a strange kind of trickery involved in the writing and reading of novels, after all. You see Leo Tolstoy's name on the cover of *War and Peace*, but once you open the book, Leo Tolstoy disappears. It's as though no one has really written the words you're reading. I find this 'no one' terribly fascinating – for there's finally a profound truth to it. On the one hand, it's an illusion: on the other hand, it has everything to do with how stories are written. For the author of a novel can never be sure where any of it comes from. The self that exists in the world – the self whose name appears on the covers of books – is finally not the same self who writes the book.

SG: *And of course it turns out that the 'Paul Auster' whom Quinn visits in the novel isn't the author of the book we've been reading – which literalizes this idea.*

PA: Right. Paul Auster appears as a character in *City of Glass*, but in the end the reader learns that he is not the author. It's someone else, an anonymous narrator who comes in on the last page and walks off with Quinn's red notebook. So the Auster on the cover and the Auster in the story are not the same person. They're the same and yet not the same. Just as the author of *War and Peace* is both Tolstoy and not Tolstoy.

LM: *Was there a specific incident or impulse that started* City of Glass?

PA: About a year after my first marriage broke up, I moved to an apartment in Brooklyn. It was early 1980, and I was working on 'The Book of Memory' then – and also editing an anthology of twentieth-century French poetry for Random House. One day, a couple of months after I moved in, the telephone rang, and the person on the other end asked if he had reached Pinkerton Agency. I said no, you've got the wrong number, and hung up. I probably would have forgotten all about it, but the very next day another person called and asked the same question. 'Is this the Pinkerton Agency?' Again I said no, told him he'd dialed the wrong number, and hung up. But the instant after I hung up, I began to wonder what would have happened if I had said yes. Would it have been possible for me to pose as a Pinkerton agent? And if so, how far could I have taken it? The book grew out of those telephone calls, but more than a year went by before I actually began to write it. The wrong numbers were the starting point, but there's no question that they influenced some of the other elements of the book as well – the private detective element, for example, and the idea of involving myself in the action of the story.

LM: *There's a scene in* City of Glass *where Quinn says that writing his Max Work mystery novels under the pen name of William Wilson made him feel he was writing these books at one step removed, so that 'Wilson served as a kind of ventriloquist. Quinn himself was the dummy, and Work was the animated voice that gave purpose to the enterprise.' Since I know that you also wrote a detective novel under a pseudonym, I was wondering if you shared some of Quinn's feelings about this process.*

PA: It was exactly the same. All through the months I

worked on that book, I felt as though I were writing with a mask on my face. It was an odd experience, but I can't say that it was unenjoyable. Posing as someone else was quite a bit of fun, in fact – but at the same time disturbing and provocative. If I hadn't gone through that experience of pseudonymity myself, I never would have been able to develop Quinn in the way I did.

SG: *You must have had mixed feelings about finding yourself labeled so often (at least initially) as a 'detective writer'.*

PA: Yes, I must say I've found it rather galling at times. Not that I have anything against detective fiction – it's just that my work has very little to do with it. I refer to it in the three novels of the *Trilogy*, of course, but only as a means to an end, as a way to get somewhere else entirely. If a true follower of detective fiction ever tried to read one of those books, I'm sure he would be bitterly disappointed. Mystery novels always give answers; my work is about asking questions.

In the long run, it probably doesn't matter. People can say whatever they want; they're entitled to misread books in any way they choose. It takes time for the dust to settle, and every writer has to be prepared to listen to a lot of stupidities when his work is discussed. The reviewing situation is particularly bad here after all. Not only do we have the worst infant mortality rate in the western world, but we probably have the lowest standard of literary journalism anywhere. Some of the people who review books strike me as quasi-illiterate, out-and-out morons. And theirs are the opinions that circulate, at least at the beginning of a book's life.

SG: *And yet, there are certain aspects about detective writing that are enormously attractive and compelling – things you point to in* City of Glass *about nothing being wasted in a good*

mystery novel, that 'the center of the book shifts with each event
that propels it forward', its potential for having everything come
to life, seething with possibilities.

PA: Of course. At its best, detective fiction can be one of
the purest and most engaging forms of story-telling. The
idea that every sentence counts, that every word can make
a difference – it creates a tremendous narrative propulsion.
It's on that level that the form has been most interesting to
me.

In the end, though, I would say that the greatest influence
on my work has been fairy tales, the oral tradition of story-
telling. The Brothers Grimm, the Thousand and One Nights
– the kinds of stories you read out loud to children. These
are bare-bones narratives, narratives largely devoid of
details, yet enormous amounts of information are com-
municated in a very short space, with very few words.
What fairy tales prove, I think, is that it's the reader – or
the listener – who actually tells the story to himself. The
text is no more than a springboard for the imagination.
'Once upon a time there was a girl who lived with her
mother in a house at the edge of a large wood.' You don't
know what the girl looks like, you don't know what colour
the house is, you don't know if the mother is tall or short,
fat or thin, you know next to nothing. But the mind won't
allow these things to remain blank; it fills in the details
itself, it creates images based on its own memories and
experiences – which is why these stories resonate so deeply
inside us. The listener becomes an active participant in the
story.

LM: *A lot of the contemporary writers who have also acknowl-*
edged a fascination with fairy tales (I'm thinking of people like
Barth, Coover, Calvino, Borges) seem to share the sense that the
fairy tale offers a method of communicating with readers that

the novel basically ignores because it wants to provide all the details, the background, the explanation.

PA: I'd certainly agree that novel-writing has strayed very far from these open-ended structures – and from oral traditions as well. The typical novel of the past two hundred years has been crammed full of details, descriptive passages, local color – things that might be excellent in themselves, but which often have little to do with the heart of the story being told, that can actually block the reader's access to that story. I want my books to be all heart, all center, to say what they have to say in as few words as possible. This ambition seems so contrary to what most novelists are trying to accomplish that I often have trouble thinking of myself as a novelist at all.

SG: *In 'The Book of Memory' you described your reaction to the breakup of your first marriage and your separation from your son by saying, 'Each day would drag a little more of the pain out into the open.' Was writing* City of Glass *one way for you to work through (or at least get at) that pain?*

PA: That was the emotional source of the book, yes. My first wife and I split up in 1979, and for a year-and-a-half after that I lived in a kind of limbo – first on Varick Street in Manhattan, then in that apartment in Brooklyn. But once the arrangements were worked out, my son was with me half the time. He was just three back then, and we lived together like a couple of old bachelors. It was a strange existence, I suppose, but not without its pleasures, and I assumed that life would go on like that for a long time. Then, early in 1981 (February 23rd, to be exact, it's impossible for me to forget the date) I met Siri Hustvedt, the person I'm married to now. We took each other by storm, and nothing has ever been the same since. For the past

nine years, she's meant everything to me, absolutely everything . . .

So, by the time I started writing *City of Glass*, my life had
undergone a dramatic improvement. I was in love with an
extraordinary woman; we were living together in a new
apartment; my inner world had been utterly transformed.
In many ways, I think of *City of Glass* as an homage to Siri,
as a love letter in the form of a novel. I tried to imagine
what would have happened to me if I hadn't met her,
and what I came up with was Quinn. Perhaps my life
would have been something like his . . .

sg: *Let's talk a bit about the question of 'solitude'. It's a word
that comes up often in your works – and of course it appears in
the title of your first book of prose,* The Invention of Solitude.
*It's a concept that seems to contain a lot of different resonances
for you, both personal and aesthetic.*

pa: Yes, I suppose there's no getting rid of it. But solitude
is a rather complex term for me; it's not just a synonym
for loneliness or isolation. Most people tend to think of
solitude as a rather gloomy idea, but I don't attach any
negative connotations to it. It's a simple fact, one of the
conditions of being human, and even if we're surrounded
by others, we essentially live our lives alone: real life takes
place inside us. We're not dogs, after all. We're not driven
solely by instincts and habits; we can think, and because
we think, we're always in two places at the same time. Even
in the throes of physical passion, thoughts come pouring
through our head. At the very height of sexual arousal, a
person can be thinking about an unanswered letter on the
dining room table or about standing on a street in a foreign
city twenty years ago – or anything, anything at all . . .

What it boils down to is the old mind-body problem.
Descartes. Solipsism. Self and other, all the old philosoph-

ical questions. In the end, we know who we are because we can think about who we are. Our sense of self is formed by the pulse of consciousness within us – the endless monologue, the life-long conversation we have with ourselves. And this takes place in absolute solitude. It's impossible to know what someone else is thinking. We can only see the surfaces: the eyes, the face, the body. But we can't see another person's thoughts, can we? We can't hear them or touch them; they're utterly walled off from us.

Oliver Sacks, the neurologist, has made some astute observations about such things. Every whole person, he says, every person with a coherent identity, is in effect narrating the story of his life to himself at every moment – following the thread of his own story. For brain-damaged people, however, this thread has been snapped. And once that happens, it's no longer possible to hold yourself together.

But there's more to it than that. We live alone, yes, but at the same time everything we are comes from the fact that we have been made by others. I'm not just referring to biology – mothers and fathers, uterine birth, and so on. I'm thinking about psychology and the formation of the human personality. The infant feeding at the mother's breast looks up into the mother's eyes and sees her looking at him, and from that experience of being seen, the baby begins to learn that he is separate from his mother, that he is a person in his own right. We literally acquire a self from this process. Lacan calls it the 'mirror-stage', which strikes me as a beautiful way of putting it. Self-consciousness in adulthood is merely an extension of those early experiences. It's no longer the mother who's looking at us then – we're looking at ourselves. But we can only see ourselves because someone else has seen us first. In other words, we learn our solitude from others. In the same way that we learn language from others.

LM: *'Solitude', then, is the essential condition of being locked inside one's own head – but also something that only comes into our awareness because of other people. This sounds like a paradox . . .*

PA: It does, but I don't know how else to express it. What is so startling to me, finally, is that you don't begin to understand your connection to others until you are alone. And the more intensely you are alone, the more deeply you plunge into a state of solitude, the more deeply you feel that connection. It isn't possible for a person to isolate himself from other people. No matter how apart you might find yourself in a physical sense – whether you've been marooned on a desert island or locked up in solitary confinement – you discover that you are inhabited by others. Your language, your memories, even your sense of isolation – every thought in your head has been born from your connection with others. This is what I was trying to explore in 'The Book of Memory', to examine both sides of the word 'solitude'. I felt as though I were looking down to the bottom of myself, and what I found there was more than just myself – I found the world. That's why that book is filled with so many references and quotations, in order to pay homage to all the others inside me. On the one hand, it's a work about being alone; on the other hand, it's about community. That book has dozens of authors, and I wanted them all to speak through me. In the final analysis, 'The Book of Memory' is a collective work.

SG: *Earlier, when we were talking about your pseudonymous novel, you said you felt like you were 'wearing a mask' while writing that book. Could you talk a bit about the different relationships you have with your characters when you're writing*

a book from the first person, as opposed to a third-person perspec-
tive? For example, do you feel less that you're wearing this mask
when you're writing in the first person? Or do you feel a more
abstract relationship to all your characters?

PA: This is a fundamental question for me. Some of my
books have been written in the first person, others have
been written in the third, and in each case the entire story
has developed out of the particular narrative voice I've
chosen. Yes, obviously a novel written in the first person
is going to sound more intimate than one written in the
third person. But there's a vast range within those two
categories, and it's possible to bring the boundaries of first-
person and third-person so close to each other that they
touch, even overlap.

SG: *How does this overlap work in your own books? Do you*
mean by confusing the distinction between who the reader thinks
the narrator is and who finally is revealed to actually be telling the
story, as you did in City of Glass?

PA: That's probably where the overlap is most obvious,
because in *City of Glass* you have a book written in the third
person throughout, and then, right at the end, the narrator
appears and announces himself in the first-person – which
colors the book in retrospect somehow, turning the whole
story into a kind of oblique, first-person narrative. But I've
been interested in pursuing different ranges of effects that
can be produced with this sort of thing in most of my
books. Even in *Ghosts*, which reads something like a fable,
you feel the presence of the narrator lurking behind each
sentence. The storyteller is a part of the story, even though
he never uses the word 'I'. In the few places where he
breaks in, he always refers to himself in the plural – as if
addressing the reader directly, including him in what is
finally a very personal 'we'. *The Locked Room* is written in

the first person, but so much of it is about trying to under-stand someone else that certain sections of it are actually written in the third person. The same holds true for *In the Country of Last Things*. The little phrases that appear a few times at the beginning – 'she wrote' or 'her letter continued' – put the whole book in a third-person perspective. Some-one has read Anna Blume's book notebook; somehow or other, her letter has arrived. *Moon Palace* functions a bit like *The Locked Room* in that it's an intimate, first-person narra-tive that veers off into the third person. There are long passages in that book where Fogg literally disappears. When it comes right down to it, *The Music of Chance* is the only one of my novels that doesn't combine first- and third-person narration. It's written strictly in the third person.

LM: *Your handling of the narrative perspective in* The Music of Chance *reminded me of what we find in several of Kafka's best works – your narrator is 'outside' the character but somehow manages to convey very directly Nashe's intensely subjective, emotionally charged 'inner' life. It's a delicate balance: the seem-ingly objective representation of an emotionally charged, psycho-logical landscape.*

PA: Yes, that third person is so close to the first person, is so deeply imagined from Nashe's point of view, that there's hardly any difference at all. It was a very wrenching experi-ence to write that book – utterly grueling and exhausting. For weeks after I finished it, I felt like a dead man.

LM: *You chose to present the two sections of* The Invention of Solitude *through two different narrative perspectives, with 'Portrait of an Invisible Man' being written in the first person, while 'The Book of Memory' is in the third person. What was involved in that choice?*

PA: The opening part was written very naturally in the first person. I didn't question it; it just came to me that way, and I went with it. When I started the next section, I assumed it would be written in the first person as well. I worked on it for six or eight months in that form but something about it disturbed me, something wasn't right. Eventually, after groping in the dark with it for a long time, I understood that the book could only be written in the third person. Rimbaud: 'Je est un autre.' It opened a door for me, and after that I worked in a kind of fever, as though my brain had caught fire.

What it came down to was creating a distance between myself and myself. If you're too close to the thing you're trying to write about, the perspective vanishes, and you begin to smother. I had to objectify myself in order to explore my own subjectivity – which gets us back to what we were talking about before: the multiplicity of the singular. The moment I think about the fact that I'm saying 'I', I'm actually saying 'he'. It's the mirror of self-consciousness, a way of watching yourself think.

SG: *Were there any particular difficulties in writing from a woman's perspective, as you did with Anna in* In the Country of Last Things?

PA: Not really. But something in me resisted it for a long time. In many ways, writing that book was like taking dictation. I *heard* her voice speaking to me – and that voice was utterly distinct from my own. In that sense, there was almost no difficulty at all.

But when you consider that I first heard that voice in 1970 and didn't finish the book until 1985, it's safe to conclude that it was a very difficult book to write. I didn't want to do it. I felt it was presumptuous to write from the viewpoint of a woman, and so every time I started working on it again, I'd stop. I'd cross my fingers and hope that the voice had talked itself out, that at last I'd be free of it. A year or two would go by, and then I'd start hearing her again. I'd write for a while, then stop again. This went on for years and years. Finally, some time in the early Eighties, right when I was in the middle of *The New York Trilogy* (I think I was between the second and third books), she came back to me in full force, and I wrote the first thirty or forty pages as they stand now. Still not sure of myself, I showed them to Siri and asked her what she thought. She said those pages were the best work I had ever done and that I had to finish the book. I had to finish the book as a present to her. 'It's my book,' she said, and she's continued to refer to it in that way ever since.

Still, there was a pause after writing those initial pages. I wanted to finish the *Trilogy* first, so more time went by before I returned to it. But in that interval, I published what I had already written in *The Paris Review*. It's the only time I've ever published a piece of a novel, but in this case it seemed to make sense. I did it as a kind of promise to myself, as a guarantee that I would actually finish it.

LM: *There's an obvious way that* In the Country of Last Things *is grounded in the dystopian or post-holocaust tradition of science fiction. But I was mostly struck with how palpably real this urban nightmare scene is. It seems not too different, in fact, from what you can find right here in New York.*

PA: As far as I'm concerned, the book has nothing to do with science fiction. It's quite fantastical at times, of course, but that doesn't mean it's not firmly anchored in historical realities. It's a novel about the present and the immediate past, not about the future. 'Anna Blume walks through the twentieth century'. That's the phrase I carried around in my head while I was working on the book.

LM: *What sorts of historical realities do you mean – the massive devastations caused in the two world wars?*

PA: Among other things, yes. There are specific references to the Warsaw ghetto and the siege of Leningrad, but also to events taking place in the Third World today – not to speak of New York, which is rapidly turning into a Third World city before our eyes. The garbage system, which I describe at such great length in the novel, is loosely based on the present-day garbage system in Cairo. All in all, there's very little invented material in the book. The characters, yes, but not the circumstances. Even the pivotal event in the story – when Anna, hoping to buy a pair of shoes, is lured into a human slaughterhouse – even that scene is based on historical fact. Precisely that kind of thing happened in Leningrad in World War II. The city was surrounded by the Germans for two and a half years, and in that time 500,000 people lost their lives. 500,000 people in one city. Just stop for a moment and try to imagine what it must have been like. Once you begin to think about such things, it's difficult to think about anything else.

I realize that many people found this book depressing, but there's nothing I can do about that. In the end, I find it the most hopeful book I've ever written. Anna Blume survives, at least to the extent that her words survive. Even in the midst of the most brutal realities, the most terrible social conditions, she struggles to remain a human being, to keep her humanity intact. I can't imagine anything more noble and courageous than that. It's a struggle that millions of people have had to face in our time, and not many of them have been as tenacious as she is. I think of Anna Blume as a true heroine.

SG: *Earlier in the interview you referred to yourself as basically an 'intuitive writer' in terms of the way your writing process operates. Maybe we could discuss the relationship between your conscious intentionality versus your intuition by talking about the way a specific image in your work develops. For instance the moon image in* Moon Palace *appears in dozens of different contexts that occasionally dovetail or coalesce into groupings – Barber's legends of the Indians (with their origins on the moon), the way the Utah desert is described as a lunar landscape, the fortune cookie that says, 'The sun is the past, the earth is the present, the moon is the future' (and which turns out to be a quote from Tesla), the restaurant named 'Moon Palace', and so on. Is the unfolding of these connections and resonances the product of conscious design or happy accident?*

PA: If you think about any one thing long enough or hard enough, it's going to begin to reverberate for you. Once that happens, waves are emitted, and those waves travel through space and bounce off other things, which in turn emit their own waves. It's an associative process, and if you stick with it conscientiously enough, large portions of the world will eventually be touched by your thoughts. It's not really a question of accident or design. This is the way the mind works. It just happens, but you have to be watching attentively for it to go on happening. Pick any object in front of you – a coffee cup, or a box of cigars, or a telephone – and try to think about where it comes from. Within ten minutes, you're onto any number of other things – geology, history, labor problems, biology, God knows what – a whole range of subjects. 'To see the world in a grain of sand.' If you're capable of doing that, imagine how much can be seen in the moon!

LM: *There's also a certain sense in which those elaborate connections and metaphorical associations being developed grow naturally out of the kind of sensibility you project for Fogg.*

PA: Precisely. Fogg is a bookish young man, an intellectual, and he has a penchant for this kind of thing. It's something he inherits from his Uncle Victor, a man who is constantly searching the world for hidden connections. The moon imagery comes from Fogg – I wasn't trying to impose it on him. At the same time, remember, he's telling the story of his youth from the distance of middle age, and he often pokes fun at himself. He's looking back on the way he *used* to think, the way he *used* to interpret the world. It's one of the many follies of his adolescence, a symptom of the madness of those times. But Fogg is a unique case. Other characters I've written about have none of these tendencies; they don't indulge in such elaborate mental gymnastics. Nashe, for example, the hero of *The Music of Chance*, has nothing in common with Fogg. He's a much more straightforward kind of person, and consequently the book he appears in is a much simpler story.

LM: *Let's go back for a second to your comment about seeing the world in a grain of sand. What made it seem so much a part of what you were doing in the novel? And how did this fit in with the 'follies' of Fogg's adolescence?*

PA: The moon is many things all at once, a touchstone. It's the moon as myth, as 'radiant Diana, image of all that is dark within us'; the imagination, love, madness. At the same time, it's the moon as object, as celestial body, as lifeless stone hovering in the sky. But it's also the longing for what is not, the unattainable, the human desire for transcendence. And yet it's history as well, particularly American history. First there's Columbus, then there was the discovery of the West, then finally there is outer space: the moon as the last frontier. But Columbus had no idea that he'd discovered America. He thought he had sailed to India, to China. In some sense, *Moon Palace* is the embodiment of that misconception, an attempt to think of America as China. But the moon is also repetition, the cyclical nature of human experience. There are three stories in the book, after all, and each one is finally the same. Each generation repeats the mistakes of the previous generation. So it's also a critique of the notion of progress. And if America is the land of progress, what are we to make of ourselves then? And so on and so on and so on. Fogg wends his way among all these ideas, this pinball machine of associations, struggling to find a place for himself. By the end of the book I think he manages to get somewhere. But he only reaches the beginning, the brink of his adult life. And that's where we leave him – getting ready to begin.

sg: *You've described how emotionally exhausting it was for you to write your latest novel,* The Music of Chance. *Did you realize when you started it that it was going to be such a wrenching book to write?*

pa: It's never possible to predict what it's going to be like. With my other books, I've usually known the general shape of the story before beginning to write it, but in this case a number of crucial elements were altered as I went along. I began with a different ending in mind, but at a certain point I realized that I had been wrong, that the book was heading for a much darker conclusion than I had originally planned. This revelation came as a shock to me, it stopped me cold in my tracks. But there was no getting around it, and after thinking it over for several days, I understood that I had no choice.

sg: *Do you recall what the origins of the book were?*

pa: At the end of *Moon Palace,* Fogg is driving out west in a car. The car is stolen, and he winds up continuing the journey on foot. I realized that I wanted to get back inside that car, to give myself a chance to go on driving around America. So there was that very immediate and visceral impulse, which is how *The Music of Chance* begins – with Nashe sitting behind the wheel of a car.

At the same time, I wanted to explore the implications of the windfall I had received after my father's death – which is something we discussed before. This led me to start thinking about the question of freedom, which is ultimately the true subject of the book.

As for the wall – those stones had been standing inside me for years. The play that I mentioned earlier, the one that was performed in the Seventies, was about two men building a wall. The whole play consists of them lugging stones around the stage, and by the end they're completely blocked off from the audience. I was never satisfied by it, but at the same time I couldn't get rid of the idea. It plagued me and haunted me for all those years. So this was my attempt to improve on what I had done with it the first time. Those are three elements of the novel that I was able to think about before I wrote it. The conscious material, so to speak. Everything else is shrouded in obscurity.

When I was about two-thirds of the way through the first draft, it occurred to me that the story had the same structure as a fairy tale. Up until then, I had only thought about the book in concrete terms, the reality of the action. But if you reduce the book to its skeleton, then you wind up with something that resembles a typical story by the Brothers Grimm, don't you? A wanderer stumbles onto an opportunity to make his fortune; he travels to the ogre's castle to test his luck, is tricked into staying there, and can win his freedom only by performing a series of absurd tasks that the ogre invents for him.

I don't know if I want to make too much out of this, but it was an interesting discovery anyway. Another example of how elusive the whole activity of writing is. Yet another testimony to my own ignorance.

1989–90

IV

A Prayer for Salman Rushdie

When I sat down to write this morning, the first thing I did was think of Salman Rushdie. I have done this every morning for almost four and a half years, and by now it is an essential part of my daily routine. I pick up my pen, and before I begin to write, I think of my fellow novelist across the ocean. I pray that he will go on living another twenty-four hours. I pray that his English protectors will keep him hidden from the people who are out to murder him – the same people who have already killed one of his translators and wounded another. Most of all, I pray that a time will come when these prayers are no longer necessary, when Salman Rushdie will be as free to walk the streets of the world as I am.

I pray for this man every morning, but deep down, I know that I am also praying for myself. His life is in danger because he wrote a book. Writing books is my business as well, and I know that if not for the quirks of history and pure blind luck, I could be in his shoes. If not today, then perhaps tomorrow. We belong to the same club: a secret fraternity of solitaries, shut-ins, and cranks, men and women who spend the better part of our time locked up in little rooms struggling to put words on a page. It is a strange way to live one's life, and only a person who had no choice in the matter would choose it as a calling. It is too arduous, too underpaid, too full of disappointments to be fit for anyone else. Talents vary, ambitions vary, but any

writer worth his salt will tell you the same thing: To write
a work of fiction, one must be free to say what one has to
say. I have exercised that freedom with every word I have
written – and so has Salman Rushdie. That is what makes
us brothers, and that is why his predicament is also mine.

I can't know how I would act in his place, but I can
imagine it – or at least I can try to imagine it. In all honesty,
I'm not sure I would be capable of the courage he has
shown. The man's life is in ruins, and yet he has continued
to do the thing he was born to do. Shunted from one
safe-house to another, cut off from his son, surrounded by
security police, he has continued to go to his desk every
day and write. Knowing how difficult it is to do this even
under the best of circumstances, I can only stand in awe of
what he has accomplished. A novel; another novel in the
works; a number of extraordinary essays and speeches
defending the basic human right to free expression. All
that is remarkable enough, but what truly astonishes me
is that on top of this essential work, he has taken the time
to review other people's books – in some cases even to
write blurbs promoting the books of unknown authors. Is
it possible for a man in his position to think of anyone but
himself? Yes, apparently it is. But I wonder how many of
us could do what he has done with our backs against that
same wall.

Salman Rushdie is fighting for his life. The struggle has
gone on for nearly half a decade, and we are no closer to
a solution than when the *fatwa* was first announced. Like
so many others, I wish there was something I could do to
help. Frustration mounts, despair sets in, but given that I
have neither the power nor the influence to affect the
decisions of foreign governments, the most I can do is pray
for him. He is carrying the burden for all of us, and I can
no longer think of what I do without thinking of him. His

plight has focused my concentration, has made me re-examine my beliefs, has taught me never to take the freedom I enjoy for granted. For all that, I owe him an immense debt of gratitude. I support Salman Rushdie in his struggle to win back his life, but the truth is that he has also supported me. I want to thank him for that. Every time I pick up my pen, I want to thank him.

1993

V

Why Write?

1

A German friend tells of the circumstances that preceded the births of her two daughters.

Nineteen years ago, hugely pregnant and already several weeks past due, A. sat down on the sofa in her living room and turned on the television set. As luck would have it, the opening credits of a film were just coming on screen. It was *The Nun's Story*, a 1950s Hollywood drama starring Audrey Hepburn. Glad for the distraction, A. settled in to watch the movie and immediately got caught up in it. Halfway through, she went into labor. Her husband drove her to the hospital, and she never learned how the film turned out.

Three years later, pregnant with her second child, A. sat down on the sofa and turned on the television set once again. Once again a film was playing, and once again it was *The Nun's Story* with Audrey Hepburn. Even more remarkable (and A. was very emphatic about this point), she had tuned into the film at the precise moment where she had left off three years earlier. This time she was able to see the film through to the end. Less than fifteen minutes later, her water broke, and she went off to the hospital to give birth for the second time.

These two daughters are A.'s only children. The first labor was extremely difficult (my friend nearly didn't make it and was ill for many months afterward), but the second delivery went smoothly, with no complications of any kind.

2

Five years ago, I spent the summer with my wife and children in Vermont, renting an old, isolated farmhouse on the top of a mountain. One day, a woman from the next town stopped by to visit with her two children, a girl of four and a boy of eighteen months. My daughter Sophie had just turned three, and she and the girl enjoyed playing with each other. My wife and I sat down in the kitchen with our guest, and the children ran off to amuse themselves.

Five minutes later, there was a loud crash. The little boy had wandered into the front hall at the other end of the house, and since my wife had put a vase of flowers in that hall just two hours earlier, it wasn't difficult to guess what had happened. I didn't even have to look to know that the floor was covered with broken glass and pools of water – along with the stems and petals of a dozen scattered flowers.

I was annoyed. Goddamn kids, I said to myself. Goddamn people with their goddamn clumsy kids. Who gave them the right to drop by without calling first?

I told my wife that I'd clean up the mess, and so while she and our visitor continued their conversation, I gathered up a broom, a dustpan, and some towels and marched off to the front of the house.

My wife had put the flowers on a wooden trunk that sat

just below the staircase railing. This staircase was especially steep and narrow, and there was a large window not more than a yard from the bottom step. I mention this geography because it's important. Where things were has everything to do with what happened next.

I was about half-finished with the clean-up job when my daughter rushed out from her room onto the second-floor landing. I was close enough to the foot of the stairs to catch a glimpse of her (a couple of steps back and she would have been blocked from view), and in that brief moment I saw that she had that high-spirited, utterly happy expression on her face that has filled my middle age with such over-powering gladness. Then, an instant later, before I could even say hello, she tripped. The toe of her sneaker had caught on the landing, and just like that, without any cry or warning, she was sailing through the air. I don't mean to suggest that she was falling or tumbling or bouncing down the steps. I mean to say that she was flying. The impact of the stumble had literally launched her into space, and from the trajectory of her flight I could see that she was heading straight for the window.

What did I do? I don't know what I did. I was on the wrong side of the bannister when I saw her trip, but by the time she was midway between the landing and the window, I was standing on the bottom step of the staircase. How did I get there? It was no more than a question of several feet, but it hardly seems possible to cover that dis-tance in that amount of time – which is next to no time at all. Nevertheless, I was there, and the moment I got there I looked up, opened my arms, and caught her.

I was fourteen. For the third year in a row, my parents had sent me to a summer camp in New York State. I spent the bulk of my time playing basketball and baseball, but as it was a co-ed camp, there were other activities as well: evening 'socials', the first awkward grapplings with girls, panty raids, the usual adolescent shenanigans. I also remember smoking cheap cigars on the sly, 'frenching' beds, and massive water-balloon fights.

None of this is important. I simply want to underscore what a vulnerable age fourteen can be. No longer a child, not yet an adult, you bounce back and forth between who you were and who you are about to become. In my own case, I was still young enough to think that I had a legitimate shot at playing in the Major Leagues, but old enough to be questioning the existence of God. I had read the Communist Manifesto, and yet I still enjoyed watching Saturday morning cartoons. Every time I saw my face in the mirror, I seemed to be looking at someone else.

There were sixteen or eighteen boys in my group. Most of us had been together for several years, but a couple of newcomers had also joined us that summer. One was named Ralph. He was a quiet kid without much enthusiasm for dribbling basketballs or hitting the cut-off man, and while no one gave him a particularly hard time, he had trouble blending in. He had flunked a couple of subjects that year, and most of his free periods were spent being tutored by one of the counselors. It was a little sad, and I felt sorry for him – but not too sorry, not sorry enough to lose any sleep over it.

Our counselors were all New York college students from Brooklyn and Queens. Wise-cracking basketball players, future dentists, accountants, and teachers, city kids to their very bones. Like most true New Yorkers they persisted in calling the ground the 'floor', even when all that was under their feet was grass, pebbles, and dirt. The trappings of traditional summer camp life were as alien to them as the I.R.T. is to an Iowa farmer. Canoes, lanyards, mountain climbing, pitching tents, singing around the campfire were nowhere to be found in the inventory of their concerns. They could drill us on the finer points of setting picks and boxing out for rebounds, but otherwise they mostly horsed around and told jokes.

Imagine our surprise, then, when one afternoon our counselor announced that we were going for a hike in the woods. He had been seized by an inspiration and wasn't going to let anyone talk him out of it. Enough basketball, he said. We're surrounded by nature, and it's time we took advantage of it and started acting like real campers – or words to that effect. And so, after the rest period that followed lunch, the whole gang of sixteen or eighteen boys along with two or three counselors set off into the woods.

It was late July, 1961. Everyone was in a fairly buoyant mood, I remember, and half an hour or so into the trek most people agreed that the outing had been a good idea. No one had a compass, of course, or the slightest clue as to where we were going, but we were all enjoying ourselves, and if we happened to get lost, what difference would that make? Sooner or later, we'd find our way back.

Then it began to rain. At first it was barely noticeable, a few light drops falling between the leaves and branches, nothing to worry about. We walked on, unwilling to let a little water spoil our fun, but a couple of minutes later it started coming down in earnest. Everyone got soaked, and the counselors decided we should turn around and head back. The only problem was that no one knew where the camp was. The woods were thick, dense with clusters of trees and thorn-studded bushes, and we had woven our way this way and that, abruptly shifting directions in order to move on. To add to the confusion, it was becoming hard to see. The woods were dark to begin with, but with the rain falling and the sky turning black, it felt more like night than three or four in the afternoon

Then the thunder started. And after the thunder, the lightning started. The storm was directly on top of us, and it turned out to be the summer storm to end all summer storms. I have never seen weather like that before or since. The rain poured down on us so hard that it actually hurt; each time the thunder exploded, you could feel the noise vibrating inside your body. Immediately after that, the lightning would come, dancing around us like spears. It was as if weapons had materialized out of thin air: a sudden flash that turned everything a bright, ghostly white. Trees were struck, and the branches would begin to smolder. Then it would go dark again for a moment, there would be another crash in the sky, and the lightning would return in a different spot.

The lightning was what scared us, of course. It would have been stupid not to be scared, and in our panic we tried to run away from it. But the storm was too big, and everywhere we went we were met by more lightning. It was a helter-skelter stampede, a headlong rush in circles. Then, suddenly, someone spotted a clearing in the woods. A brief dispute broke out over whether it was safer to go into the open or continue to stand under the trees. The voice arguing for the open won, and we all ran in the direction of the clearing.

It was a small meadow, most likely a pasture that belonged to a local farm, and to get to it we had to crawl under a barbed-wire fence. One by one, we got down on our bellies and inched our way through. I was in the middle of the line, directly behind Ralph. Just as he went under the barbed wire, there was another flash of lightning. I was two or three feet away, but because of the rain pounding against my eyelids, I had trouble making out what happened. All I knew was that Ralph had stopped moving. I figured that he had been stunned, so I crawled past him under the fence. Once I was on the other side, I took hold of his arm and dragged him through.

I don't know how long we stayed in that field. An hour, I would guess, and the whole time we were there the rain and thunder and lightning continued to crash down upon us. It was a storm ripped from the pages of the Bible, and it went on and on and on, as if it would never end.

Two or three boys were hit by something – perhaps by lightning, perhaps by the shock of lightning as it struck the ground near them – and the meadow began to fill with their moans. Other boys wept and prayed. Still others, fear in their voices, tried to give sensible advice. Get rid of everything metal, they said, metal attracts the lightning. We all took off our belts and threw them away from us.

I don't remember saying anything. I don't remember crying. Another boy and I kept ourselves busy trying to take care of Ralph. He was still unconscious. We rubbed his hands and arms, we held down his tongue so he wouldn't swallow it, we told him to hang in there. After a while, his skin began to take on a bluish tinge. His body seemed colder to my touch, but in spite of the mounting evidence, it never once occurred to me that he wasn't going to come around. I was only fourteen years old, after all, and what did I know? I had never seen a dead person before.

It was the barbed wire that did it, I suppose. The other boys hit by the lightning went numb, felt pain in their limbs for an hour or so, and then recovered. But Ralph had been under the fence when the lightning struck, and he had been electrocuted on the spot.

Later on, when they told me he was dead, I learned that there was an eight-inch burn across his back. I remember trying to absorb this news and telling myself that life would never feel the same to me again. Strangely enough, I didn't think about how I had been right next to him when it happened. I didn't think, One or two seconds later, and it would have been me. What I thought about was holding his tongue and looking down at his teeth. His mouth had been set in a slight grimace, and with his lips partly open, I had spent an hour looking down at the tips of his teeth. Thirty-four years later, I still remember them. And his half-closed, half-open eyes. I remember those, too.

4

Not many years ago, I received a letter from a woman who lives in Brussels. In it, she told me the story of a friend of hers, a man she has known since childhood.

In 1940, this man joined the Belgian Army. When the country fell to the Germans later that year, he was captured and put in a prisoner-of-war camp. He remained there until the war ended in 1945.

Prisoners were allowed to correspond with Red Cross workers back in Belgium. The man was arbitrarily assigned a pen pal – a Red Cross nurse from Brussels – and for the next five years he and this woman exchanged letters every month. Over the course of time they became fast friends. At a certain point (I'm not exactly sure how long this took), they understood that something more than friendship had developed between them. The correspondence went on, growing more intimate with each exchange, and at last they declared their love for each other. Was such a thing possible? They had never seen each other, had never spent a minute in each other's company.

After the war was over, the man was released from prison and returned to Brussels. He met the nurse, the nurse met him, and neither was disappointed. A short time later, they were married.

Years went by. They had children, they grew older, the

world became a slightly different world. Their son completed his studies in Belgium and went off to do graduate work in Germany. At the university there, he fell in love with a young German woman. He wrote his parents and told them that he intended to marry her.

The parents on both sides couldn't have been happier for their children. The two families arranged to meet, and on the appointed day the German family showed up at the house of the Belgian family in Brussels. As the German father walked into the living room and the Belgian father rose to welcome him, the two men looked into each other's eyes and recognized each other. Many years had passed, but neither one was in any doubt as to who the other was. At one time in their lives, they had seen each other every day. The German father had been a guard in the prison camp where the Belgian father had spent the war.

As the woman who wrote me the letter hastened to add, there was no bad blood between them. However monstrous the German regime might have been, the German father had done nothing during those five years to turn the Belgian father against him.

Be that as it may, these two men are now the best of friends. The greatest joy in both their lives is the grandchildren they have in common.

5

I was eight years old. At that moment in my life, nothing was more important to me than baseball. My team was the New York Giants, and I followed the doings of those men in the black and orange caps with all the devotion of a true believer. Even now, remembering that team which no longer exists, that played in a ball park which no longer exists, I can reel off the names of nearly every player on the roster. Alvin Dark, Whitey Lockman, Don Mueller, Johnny Antonelli, Monte Irvin, Hoyt Wilhelm. But none was greater, none more perfect nor more deserving of worship than Willie Mays, the incandescent Say-Hey Kid.

That spring, I was taken to my first big league game. Friends of my parents had box seat seats at the Polo Grounds, and one April night a group of us went to watch the Giants play the Milwaukee Braves. I don't know who won, I can't recall a single detail of the game, but I do remember that after the game was over my parents and their friends sat talking in their seats until all the other spectators had left. It got so late that we had to walk across the diamond and leave by the center-field exit, which was the only one still open. As it happened, that exit was right below the players' locker rooms.

Just as we approached the wall, I caught sight of Willie Mays. There was no question about who it was. It was

Willie Mays, already out of uniform and standing there in his street clothes not ten feet away from me. I managed to keep my legs moving in his direction and then, mustering every ounce of my courage, I forced some words out of my mouth. 'Mr Mays,' I said, 'could I please have your autograph?'

He had to have been all of twenty-four years old, but I couldn't bring myself to pronounce his first name.

His response to my question was brusque but amiable. 'Sure, kid, sure,' he said. 'You got a pencil?' He was so full of life, I remember, so full of youthful energy, that he kept bouncing up and down as he spoke.

I didn't have a pencil, so I asked my father if I could borrow his. He didn't have one either. Nor did my mother. Nor, as it turned out, did any of the other grown-ups.

The great Willie Mays stood there watching in silence. When it became clear that no one in the group had anything to write with, he turned to me and shrugged. 'Sorry , kid,' he said. 'Ain't got no pencil, can't give no autograph.' And then he walked out of the ballpark into the night.

I didn't want to cry, but tears started falling down my cheeks, and there was nothing I could do to stop them. Even worse, I cried all the way home in the car. Yes, I was crushed with disappointment, but I was also revolted at myself for not being able to control those tears. I wasn't a baby. I was eight years old, and big kids weren't supposed to cry over things like that. Not only did I not have Willie Mays's autograph, I didn't have anything else either. Life had put me to the test, and in all respects I had found myself wanting.

After that night, I started carrying a pencil with me wherever I went. It became a habit of mine never to leave the house without making sure I had a pencil in my pocket. It's not that I had any particular plans for that pencil, but I didn't want to be unprepared. I had been caught empty-handed once, and I wasn't about to let it happen again.

If nothing clsc, the years have taught me this: if there's a pencil in your pocket, there's a good chance that one day you'll feel tempted to start using it.

As I like to tell my children, that's how I became a writer.

1995